COL Jimmie Dean Coy (Ret)

Joshua 24.15

"My faith is the source of every combat medal I ever received. Faith is the bedrock of courage. Jim Coy carries this message so well in this book and all his books. I highly recommend it to all who love their country and especially our warriors, those who protect our nation."
—*MG Pat Brady, USA (Ret) MOH, Vietnam.*

"Because of my faith and love for my Savior and Lord Jesus Christ, I would like to encourage everyone to read this devotional. I have known my brother in Christ, Jim Coy, for some time, and the love that I have for my country and its defenders is reaffirmed as I read the book, *Those Who Serve*. I highly recommend it to my Christian brothers and sisters."
—*Rudy Hernandez, MOH, Korea*

"*Those Who Serve* is like a cup of cold water in the desert. The book offers refreshment and life sustenance for the spirit of the one who reads it. My friend and fellow soldier, Jim Coy, has provided the much needed help to soldiers for guidance in communication with spiritual authority in our lives. I recommend the book, along with study of the Bible, at every opportunity for daily devotions."
—*Bob Maxwell, MOH, WWII*

"I have been blessed to know Jim Coy many years as he continues to author more books honoring the Lord and those in the military. This book combines service to the Lord and to the nation and makes it easy to share and encourage a faith in God. The book is a great resource for all who have a love of God and nation."
—*Col. Leo Thorsness, USAF (Ret) MOH Vietnam*

"Jim Coy is an author who understands the relationship between physical and moral courage and the true source of honor. His own noble standards are part of the greatness of this and his other books."
—*RADM Jeremiah Denton, USN, (Ret), Former U.S. Senator and Ex-POW, Vietnam*

"Any book written by this red, white, and blue Christian author will make a powerful and positive impact on the reader. Everyone who reads it will experience a renewed awareness of what makes America the greatest nation in the world."
—*Brig Gen Robbie Risner, USAF, (Ret), Ace Korean War, Ex-POW, Vietnam*

Those Who SERVE

A Gathering of Eagles, Book Four

A Devotional for the Military

COL Jimmie Dean Coy (Ret.)

Evergreen PRESS

The publisher wishes to thank the Congressional Medal of Honor Society for the information obtained at their website and used and also for their valuable help by providing photographs. Their website is: www.cmohs.org and it contains a myriad of information about the Medal of Honor and its recipients.

The official citations are included as issued with only minor grammatical corrections. Military abbreviations and numerical designations were kept intact.

ISBN 978-1-58169-471-0
For Worldwide Distribution
Printed in the U.S.A.

Evergreen Press
P.O. Box 191540 • Mobile, AL 36619
800-367-8203

To all who have served,
to those who currently serve,
to those who will serve in the future,
and their families.

TABLE OF CONTENTS

Part 3—Life Stories

Part 4—Songs and Oaths

Part 5—Prisoners of Hope

Note: ETO denotes European Theater of Operations
PTO denotes Pacific Theater of Operations

INTRODUCTION

This unique devotional addresses faith, family, and freedom. It includes personal life stories from the author as well as 33 stories from Medal of Honor recipients and ex-POWs. Part of the stories are told in the inspiring companion DVD, *Those Who Serve...VALOR and PRISONERS OF HOPE.*

Most of the author's stories connect military history and examples of military insignia from many different conflicts and wars to a pertinent scripture with a biblical reference. Also included are lyrics from patriotic and faith-based songs.

LEADERSHIP

Steve Farrar is one of my favorite authors. The following story about leadership is from his book, *Point Man*.

Welcome to Vietnam. You would give anything not to be here. You are going out on patrol. You've been on patrol before, but today is different, that's why there's a knot in your gut and an icy fear in your heart.

Today the patrol leader has appointed you to be the "point man." You're the leader. Everyone else will fall in behind you. You realize the survival of those men behind will depend upon your ability to lead. Your judgment may determine whether they live or die.

As you make your way through the rain forest, you've got one eye out for concealed wires in your path and another scanning the trees for snipers. Entire patrols have been lost because the point man failed to anticipate an ambush. Men have been killed or maimed, all because a point man lacked skill and wisdom.

You never saw it coming. The shock and utter surprise of gunfire momentarily paralyzes you. A bullet tears through your flesh. In the chaos of the attack, and in spite of your wounds, the radio man makes his way to you. He knows and you know that you are the most experienced and you are the leader.

As a medic evaluates your wound, you're trying to determine what to do next. You get on the radio and report your situation and position. You request a chopper for the wounded. But before you can finish your request, the hidden enemy unleashes all of his firepower on your position. You're surrounded.

In your gut you know the odds are against you. You're outnumbered, outgunned. The worst case scenario has happened... and it's worse than you ever imagined.

Now is the time your leadership will make the difference. What you say and do will determine whether your men live or die. You must accurately assess the situation, determine the critical next steps, and formulate a flawless plan. It's leadership, pure and simple. If your plan works, you may get out alive. If it doesn't, they will be lucky to find your dog tags.

Let's make a critical change in the scenario. You're still in Vietnam, on patrol in the same steamy rain forest. But something about this patrol is different. You're still the point man, but this time you're not leading a group of men. You're leading your family.

You look over your shoulder to see your wife and your children following behind. Your little girl is trying to choke back tears, and your little boy is trying to act brave. Your wife is holding the baby and trying to keep him quiet. On this patrol, you don't want to engage the enemy, you want to avoid him.

The survival of each member of your family and its survival as a whole would completely depend upon your ability to lead through the maze of possible ambushes, unseen booby traps, snipers and all the hazards of combat. Would you be motivated? It's all on your shoulders...you are the leader.

This is no imaginary situation. It is reality. If you are a husband/father, then you are at war. War has been declared on the family. Leading a family through the chaos of American culture is like leading a patrol through enemy-occupied territory. And the casualties in this war are as real as the names etched on the Vietnam Memorial.

Excerpted from the book, *Point Man,* by Steve Farrar. Used with permission by Multnomah.

Part 1

VALOR
A Gathering of Eagles

ADVICE for LIFE, CITATIONS and STORIES
from the men who ring the cover of the book
VALOR—A GATHERING OF EAGLES

First Sergeant Nicky D. Bacon
U.S. Army (Ret.) • Vietnam

"In combat, my faith in God grew as did my respect for the word 'honor.' I wish I could sit down at a campfire with all of our nation's children, and they would listen to my words of advice. They are simple words: No one is perfect, everyone fails and often comes a little short of what we expect of ourselves.

"I have traveled the world and have seen many places and different races of people. I trained years for war and fought in the dark jungles of Vietnam. Yet, I know so little, I feel so small. I have searched for strength and found weakness. I have found the true and everlasting strength only through faith in my God. I have found that, through prayer, I am a giant of power and ability. But faith is not something that just happens, you must develop it. With faith you can move a mountain, keep a family together, help a friend, or even win a war.

"If you desire spiritual greatness, you must humble yourself, set aside all your human pride, study the Word of God, and always be in prayer."

Rank and Organization
Staff Sergeant, U.S. Army, Company B, 4th Battalion,
21st Infantry, 11th Infantry Brigade, Americal Division.
Place and date
West of Tam Ky, Republic of Vietnam, 8/26/68.

CITATION

For conspicuous gallantry and intrepidity in action at the risk of his life above and beyond the call of duty. S/Sgt. Bacon distinguished himself while serving as a squad leader with the 1st Platoon, Company B, during an operation west of Tam Ky.

When Company B came under fire from an enemy bunker line to the front, S/Sgt. Bacon quickly organized his men and led them forward in an assault. He advanced on a hostile bunker and destroyed it with grenades. As he did so, several fellow soldiers including the 1st Platoon leader, were struck by machine gun fire and fell wounded in an exposed position forward of the rest of the platoon. S/Sgt. Bacon immediately assumed command of the platoon and assaulted the hostile gun position, finally killing the enemy gun crew in a single-handed effort.

When the 3d Platoon moved to S/Sgt. Bacon's location, its leader was also wounded. Without hesitation, S/Sgt. Bacon took charge of the additional platoon and continued the fight. In the ensuing action, he personally killed 4 more enemy soldiers and silenced an antitank weapon.

Under his leadership and example, the members of both platoons accepted his authority without question. Continuing to ignore the intense hostile fire, he climbed up on the exposed deck of a tank and directed fire into the enemy position while several wounded men were evacuated.

As a result of S/Sgt. Bacon's extraordinary efforts, his company was able to move forward, eliminate the enemy positions, and rescue the men trapped at the front. S/Sgt. Bacon's bravery at the risk of his life was in the highest traditions of the military service and reflects great credit upon himself, his unit, and the U.S. Army.

NO GREATER GIFT—
A HERO'S HEART

I was born in Caraway, Arkansas—a small farming community in northeast Arkansas. Most of my family members and friends were from the same economically depressed surroundings. Cotton was king and when poor crop prices hit us hard, bad times got worse. The one thing I remember most about my younger years in the cotton fields was that although we were poor and times were hard, people were most always cheerful, trusted in God, and loved one another.

My childhood experience in hardship and my close association with a group of people who had great values and steadfast faith helped me develop a trust in God that far exceeded any faith in my own abilities. This same faith gave me confidence to overcome obstacles in life, in combat, in my profession as a soldier, and in the other difficulties that I would face.

I survived two tours in the jungles of Vietnam with combat infantry units. I have seen many great men make sacrifices to save others—men willing to die for their friends. It takes more than just love for your country or patriotism to have great courage. It takes a hero's heart, that is, a personal love for those around you because you know they would do the same for you.

On the 26th of August, 1968, while serving with B company, the 11th Light Infantry Brigade of the Americal Division, we came under heavy fire from an enemy bunker in an area near Tam Ky. We were led by a great commander and friend, Captain Treadwell, ("Big T"). Many great Americans were struck down that day: some were wounded; some died. Many were struck down trying to help me...and they called me a hero! As always during the battle, I prayed as often as possible while dodging bullets, rocket fire, and hand grenades. Why God lets some of us live and others die I will never know, but I do know this: A man can live a lifetime helping others, but no one can give more in a lifetime than my friends gave in just one moment of time.

Life and death are as close as dark and light at early dawn. We do have a purpose in life; God has designed a plan for each of us to fulfill. We can only trust in His power and greatness, and if we continue to march forward in faith, we can finish the race set before us.

—*Nick Bacon*

Gary B. Beikirch
U.S. Army • Vietnam

"I would like to share with you two of the most significant experiences in my life. My experiences in Vietnam taught me many life-changing lessons: How precious life is...how frightening death can be...and how important God is to both life and death. After being med-evaced from Vietnam, wounded three times, and spending almost a year in the hospital, I was left with questions that I could not answer, an anger I could not control, and a guilt that almost destroyed me. What I needed was my second experience.

"Two years after leaving Vietnam, a friend shared with me a simple but powerful message: God loved me.... He had forgiven me because His Son, Jesus Christ, died for me, and He wanted His Spirit to become the center of my life. God's allowing me to wear the Medal of Honor was only to open doors so I could share His love (Jer. 9:23-24; Ps. 49:20). Although this is not Scripture, the following quote had an immediate impact on me as soon as I read it. I first saw it in a Mike Force team house in Pleiku. 'To really live you must almost die. To those who fight for it...life has a meaning...the protected will never know!'"

Rank and organization
Sergeant, U.S. Army, Company B, 5th Special Forces Group,
1st Special Forces.
Place and date
Kontum Province, Republic of Vietnam, 4/1/70.

CITATION

For conspicuous gallantry and intrepidity in action at the risk of his life above and beyond the call of duty. Sgt. Beikirch, medical aidman, Detachment B-24, Company B, distinguished himself during the defense of Camp Dak Seang.

The allied defenders suffered a number of casualties as a result of an intense, devastating attack launched by the enemy from well-concealed positions surrounding the camp. Sgt. Beikirch, with complete disregard for his personal safety, moved unhesitatingly through the withering enemy fire to his fallen comrades, applied first aid to their wounds and assisted them to the medical aid station. When informed that a seriously injured American officer was lying in an exposed position, Sgt. Beikirch ran immediately through the hail of fire. Although he was wounded seriously by fragments from an exploding enemy mortar shell, Sgt. Beikirch carried the officer to a medical aid station. Ignoring his own serious injuries, Sgt. Beikirch left the relative safety of the medical bunker to search for and evacuate other men who had been injured. He was again wounded as he dragged a critically injured Vietnamese soldier to the medical bunker while simultaneously applying mouth-to-mouth resuscitation to sustain his life. Sgt. Beikirch again refused treatment and continued his search for other casualties until he collapsed. Only then did he permit himself to be treated. Sgt. Beikirch's complete devotion to the welfare of his comrades, at the risk of his life, are in keeping with the highest traditions of the military service and reflect great credit on him, his unit, and the U.S. Army.

FOR HIS HONOR

April 1, 1970...over thirty years ago but I can still hear the screams, the explosions, the gunfire. April Fools day...if only it could have been a joke...but it was not. It was painfully real.

I was a member of a Green Beret Special Forces A team in Vietnam. Our peaceful Montagnard jungle camp was surrounded by 3 North Vietnamese regiments. Inside the camp of Dak Seang were 12 Americans and 2,300 Montagnard villagers, mostly women and children. It is still their screams and lifeless bodies that I remember even today.

Artillery and rockets began pounding the camp in the early morning and continued for hours. Then the "human wave" assault of ground troops began. Our jungle home had become a scene of horror, terror, and death.

Running across an open area, I saw a wounded Montagnard (we affectionately called them "Yards") lying on the ground. As I was trying to bandage his wounds, I heard "IT" coming, like a diesel train...more artillery...maybe a 122mm rocket. As I threw my body over the wounded man to shield him from the explosion, I felt like I had been kicked in the back by a horse. Shrapnel from the blasts had slammed into my back and abdomen. The concussion from the blast had thrown me about 25 feet into a wall of sandbags by our mortar pit. I tried to get up but could not move my legs. I remember thinking, "Well, at least I'm alive...and hey! There's a Purple Heart." I looked back to see what had happened to the "Yard" I was helping and all that was left was pieces...the explosion had torn him apart. How? Why? I was lying on top of him. Why was I still alive? These questions would plague me for years, but at that moment, there was too much to do.

Two other "Yards" came by and picked me up. They wanted to take me to the medical bunker but I yelled, "No!! We've got things to do up here." For hours they carried me as we treated the wounded, dragged bodies, distributed ammo, directed fire, and fought for our lives. As I continued to lose blood, I was getting weaker. Also by this time I was wounded two more times. I finally lost consciousness. When I awoke I realized they had taken me to the underground medical bunker. Pat, a new medic who had been in camp less than a week said, "Man, you're hurt bad. We got to get you out of here." I screamed out to my "Yards": "Get me out of here. If I am going to die, I am not going to die down here." A year of living with these "Yards" had developed a strong bond of love and trust between us. It was this bond that made them pick me up and carry me back out into the battle.

As the battle raged on, my two "Yard" friends carried me for hours, taking me where I directed them, helping me care for the wounded, shielding me, protecting me, holding me up as we continued to fight. Later, I would again be plagued by the questions of, "Why did they carry me all that time? Why did they stay with me?" They never left my side. What made their love for me so strong that they were willing to give their lives for me? One was killed as he saved my life.

At some point, I finally collapsed and was unable to go on. From here on my personal memories are a swirling stream of sporadic events...watching med-evac helicopters being shot down as they tried to get me out...strong arms reaching down and pulling me into the "warm belly" of a chopper, the face of the young medic shocked at seeing that I was still alive, but telling me I was going to be OK, being thrown onto a litter and rushed into an operating room, IVs in my arms and neck, catheters in every opening of my body, lights, shouting, and then...darkness.

I awoke not knowing how long I had been unconscious. I did a quick self exam...unable to move from my waist down (I would learn later that it was only a temporary injury, a shock to my spine and spinal cord from the shrapnel injury.) "What is that on my stomach?" My large intestine was in a plastic bag (shrapnel had perforated my large intestine and a colostomy had been done). More tubes were in my body...one through my nose and in the stomach...my stomach! Why did it hurt so? I looked down and realized it had been ripped open and was now sutured back together. Then darkness...I was once again unconscious. These periods of being "in and out of consciousness" continued...each time bringing new awareness. Once, I came to and watched as an Australian advisor fought for his last breath and lost. As they pulled the sheet over his head, I began drifting into unconsciousness and wondered if this was MY death.

I awoke once again but this time my waking moments were spent battling with the deaths of so many of my friends: the "Yard" I covered with my body, the one who carried me for hours...Why am I still alive and they are not? God, I feel so guilty, so helpless, so angry.

Days passed as I continued to come and go. One day I awoke and there was a chaplain standing by the next bed praying with a young dying soldier. He turned and saw my open eyes. "Glad to see you're awake. I've been praying for you for a couple of days. Would you like to pray?" My answer to his question was a pleading, "I don't know how." He simply replied, "That doesn't matter. God knows how to listen." My prayer was a simple one: "God, I don't know if you're real. I don't know if you're here, but I'm scared and I need You."

Right then something happened...no flashes of light, no miraculous physical healing, no visions on the wall or by my bed, but a peace, a comfort, a "knowing" that there was Someone outside of myself who heard my prayer and wanted me to know that I was loved as I was never loved before.

The next two years were spent searching to find out more about this Presence, this God who had touched my life. I traveled around the country, through Canada, studied different philosophies, religions, searching for ways that might lead me once again to that Peace. My search led me to a small town on the ocean just south of Boston. I was visiting a friend and told him about Vietnam, the lessons it had taught me, the questions it had left with me, and my efforts to find God. He told me that there is no mystery to finding God. He then asked me to do him a favor and read a book. He handed me a New Testament.

As I read what Jesus taught about life, the heart of man, our need for forgiveness, and God's love for us, I knew that He was the One whom I had met in the hospital bed in Vietnam. He had seen my pain and my fear and had given me His Peace and Comfort. He also had been with me all those years as I was looking for more of that Peace. As I read more of His words I learned that He wanted me to know Him. He wanted to become a greater part of my life. He didn't want me to know about Him, He wanted me to KNOW HIM, to walk with Him, to love Him, and allow Him to love me.

After my discharge from the Army, I had planned on going to medical school. However, once I started walking with my new "Friend," I felt like He wanted me to do something different. I packed my bags, headed for Florida with a Bible, and stayed there for a couple of months praying and asking God what He wanted me to do. His answer to me was to go into the ministry.

In September of 1973, I entered seminary, dedicating my life to serving the God who had given me life. One night a few weeks later I received a phone call from Washington, D.C. asking me to come to Washington and be presented the Congressional Medal of Honor by President Nixon. Coincidence? I do not believe in coincidences any more...not when you are walking with God. However, among many other emotions, I was also very confused. I knew I was not worthy of such an honor. God knew I wasn't worthy. But as I looked to Him for the reason, I believe He presented the honor to me so that it might "open doors" and allow others to hear about His desire to have a personal relationship with us through His Son, Jesus Christ.

God does have a plan and a purpose for our lives, and although there is no mystery to finding Him, at times it is a mystery to walk with Him. It wasn't easy for me at first. Even now there are times when I fail to trust His love completely, but then I remember my two "Yard" friends who loved me, protected me, and carried me when I couldn't walk. If I could trust them with my life, why shouldn't I be able to trust Jesus?

So each day I trust and walk humbly with Him...and I wear the Medal of Honor for Him and my two "Yard" friends.

—*Gary Beikirch*

Major General Patrick Brady
U.S. Army (Ret.) • Vietnam

"I believe you will agree with me that there is one virtue that is key to all others for it secures them—courage. No other virtue, not freedom, not justice, not anything, not anyone, is safe without courage. Courage then, both physical and moral, is also the first trait of leadership.

"I believe the key to courage is faith. In combat, I coped with fear through my faith. It's a great source of calm, of comfort, and it gave me great confidence. I think because of my faith I was able to do things that, for me, would have otherwise been impossible."

———◆◆◆◆◆———

Rank and organization
Major, U.S. Army, Medical Service Corps, 54th Medical Detachment, 67th Medical Group, 44th Medical Brigade.
Place and date
Near Chu Lai, Republic of Vietnam, 1/6/68.

CITATION

For conspicuous gallantry and intrepidity in action at the risk of his life above and beyond the call of duty, Maj. Brady distinguished himself while serving in the Republic of Vietnam commanding a UH-1H ambulance helicopter, volunteered to rescue wounded men from a site in enemy held territory which was reported to be heavily defended and to be blanketed by fog.

To reach the site, he descended through heavy fog and smoke and hovered slowly along a valley trail, turning his ship sideward to blow away the fog with the backwash from his rotor blades. Despite the unchallenged, close-range enemy fire, he found the dangerously small site where he successfully landed and evacuated 2 badly wounded South Vietnamese soldiers.

He was then called to another area completely covered by dense fog where American casualties lay only 50 meters from the enemy. Two aircraft had previously been shot down and others had made unsuccessful attempts to reach this site earlier in the day. With unmatched skill and extraordinary courage, Maj. Brady made 4 flights to this embattled landing zone and successfully rescued all the wounded.

On his third mission of the day, Maj. Brady once again landed at a site surrounded by the enemy. The friendly ground force, pinned down by enemy fire, had been unable to reach and secure the landing zone. Although his aircraft had been badly damaged and his controls partially shot away during his initial entry into this area, he returned minutes later and rescued the remaining injured.

Shortly thereafter, obtaining a replacement aircraft, Maj. Brady was requested to land in an enemy minefield where a platoon of American soldiers was trapped. A mine detonated near his helicopter, wounding 2 crewmembers and damaging his ship. In spite of this, he managed to fly 6 severely injured patients to medical aid.

Throughout that day, Maj. Brady utilized 3 helicopters to evacuate a total of 51 seriously wounded men, many of whom would have perished without prompt medical treatment. Maj. Brady's bravery was in the highest traditions of the military service and reflects great credit upon himself and the U.S. Army.

GOD'S LIGHT IN THE
DARKNESS AND DOUBT

In my youth, I attended 10 different schools the first 9 years of my schooling. My brothers and I were herded from relative to relative and in and out of boarding schools. We were in Catholic schools on and off and boarded with Christian Brothers of Ireland where I developed and found great comfort in my faith. Without parents or lasting friendships, the Brothers and Nuns became my mentors. I learned early on that the only lasting relationship one has is with our self and with God. Some long forgotten Brother or Nun convinced me that I always had a friend in Jesus, and just talk to Him.

I enjoyed the quiet time at Mass and Jesus became my one true friend and mentor. I got in the habit of talking through my problems with Him, not always in a prayerful way but casually in the heat of competition or what was at the time a desperate need. I do to this day. Success for me in any endeavor was based on my state of grace and my state of friendship with the Lord. If I was doing well in these areas, I knew He would listen to me.

I was a Dustoff pilot in Vietnam. Our job was to pick up the wounded from the battlefield much like 9-1-1 ambulances do from the streets of America. One in three of the Dustoff crews became a casualty in this work. More of those casualties were the result of a combination of night and weather than enemy action. Dustoff was the most effective combat operating system in that war. Survival rates of our combat troops were phenomenal and, in fact, there was a greater chance of survival if you were shot in the jungles of Vietnam than if you were in an accident on the highways of America.

During my first tour in Vietnam, most of my flying was done in the Delta, a large force landing area. There was not a lot of relief. It was mostly flat, moist terrain with few mountains. In addition, it was filled with canals connecting every possible pick-up site. Even in the roughest weather, and at night, one need only get on a canal and follow it through intersections to the patients. You could turn on your landing light, or searchlight, or both, and hover along at low-level much like driving from point to point on a highway. Day or night, it was difficult to keep us from a patient.

You can imagine my concern when I returned for a second tour, this time to the mountains of I Corps. We were in Chu Lai, just south of Danang. The terrain along the coast was flat and full of rice paddies, much like the Delta, but unfortunately it gave way inland to rugged mountainous terrain. This was where most of the fighting took place. It was an area of violent storms characterized by thick early morning fog that covered the valleys about 500 feet up the mountains. In the afternoons you could expect the tops of the mountains, key military terrain, to be covered with clouds about 500 feet down. This was the type of weather and terrain that killed so many of my fellow Dustoff crewmembers.

My concern was heightened by the fact that all but two of the pilots in the unit were right out of flight school with no experience in combat. There was nothing in flight school to match the challenges they would face in this terrain and the intensity of combat that existed upon our arrival. In fact, all six of our aircraft were damaged by enemy fire on one day in the first week we were operational. Of the 40 men in this detachment, 23 would get Purple Heart medals within 10 months. But it wasn't the enemy that concerned me as we moved the unit from Fort Benning and began to set up operations at Chu Lai. There was no way to avoid him. It was the weather and the mountains that terrified me.

For those who have heard the anguish of a soldier pleading for someone to come and save the life of his buddy, there is nothing else in life to equal it. The challenge was always to save that life and not kill the 4 crew members on your chopper doing it. To do this, you had to overcome the challenges of nearby enemy fire, the terrain, and the limitations of the aircraft and those operating it. And all of this had to be done in a timely manner. The troops could die if you waited for the fire or weather to lift, or for the sun to rise.

As I mentioned, the first week was murderous; several crew

members were hurt and all our aircraft damaged. But no one was killed, and we had not come face to face with night weather missions or tropical storms.

It had to happen. We got a call one evening about a soldier who was bitten by a snake at a fire support base on one of the mountains just west of Chu Lai. As I approached the area, I saw to my horror that the mountain-top was engulfed in thick clouds. As always, I turned to God for help. What in the heck did He want me to do? To fly into zero-zero weather without being on an approved flight plan on instruments to a proper let-down facility was against all flight regulations. A mishap under those conditions could end my career even if no one was hurt. I was required to turn back. By this time, the troops were on the radio screaming that the patient had gone into convulsions. They were begging for help. God gave me a hint. I knew I had to try. I started head-first up the mountain right above the trees.

The good news was that if I got disoriented, I could fall away from the mountain and I would break out in the valley. And that is what happened several times. The troops were pleading for me to help them and I was pleading with God to help me. The crew was very tense. (I had on board a new mechanic and this was his first mission. He refused to fly again after this mission.) Each time I got in the clouds I would get disoriented and, with much luck, be able to fall into the valley. On what I promised to be the last try, I really messed up. We were blown sideways and I was looking out my side window for a place to go in when I discovered that I could see the tip of my rotor blade and the tops of the trees. I had two reference points, and I knew I was right side up. Thank You, my good Lord. I turned that baby sideways and hovered up the mountain watching the blade and the treetops, right into the area. The troops were delighted, and we got the patient to the hospital. As a bonus on this mission someone said "God bless you, Double Nickel" (my call sign) on the radio. I knew God had blessed us although I was a little upset that He took what I thought was a bit too long to do it.

I did not get court-martialed and, in fact, used this technique many times for several of the missions on the day I was to receive the Medal of Honor. In the citation they said I flew sideways and blew away the fog. That was the only way they could explain it since one cannot fly visually in instrument conditions. God taught me that such is not the case. The truth is that you can see about 40 feet in the thickest stuff and if you have a second reference point, you can go anywhere, albeit slowly. Some day when you are on an airplane in the clouds look out the wing or when you are driving in the rain, compare your visibility out an open side window with the visibility out the windshield, and you will see what I mean.

We had solved the low valley fog and the mountain top cloud problem, but the night weather mission was still lurking. The call came during the night in the middle of a tropical storm. I was already sweating before we had all the information. The unit had suffered several loads of casualties in the valley beyond the mountains. Okay, Lord, what now? I started with the technique we used in the Delta and tried to stay under the weather and hover forward. I turned my searchlight on and had the crew lie on the floor and look out the door to the rear. The lights of a village were kept in sight as we hovered from light to light into the mountains.

It was pouring rain and the searchlight reflected off the rain and blinded me. It was like flying in an inkwell in front and we were losing the lights to the rear. I knew I would hit a mountain if we went any further, and it would eventually require instruments to fly. I had a bird that was not fully instrumented and that was risky. I decided to go north to a break in the mountains and see if I could follow a river down into the patient area as I had done with canals in the Delta. I was in my usual mode of conversation with God, wondering why He was doing this to me, and how He was going to help me get those patients out. I got to the river and had the same problem with the blinding rain and the searchlight. Then I had a vision. Thank you, dear Jesus.

On a previous night mission, I had flown a routine pickup into the valley that we called "Death Valley." As I sat on the ground loading the patients, I was enjoying the usual paradoxical beauty of the night on the battlefield. The flares drifted down through the mountains illuminating the beautiful landscape in light and dark multiple shades of green pierced occasionally with the deadly but beautiful mesmerizing streaks of tracer fire. I absentmindedly looked up and noticed that one of the mountains was covered with clouds but in perfect silhouette from the flares.

The vision came back to me, and I now knew how to get those guys out. I called back to the base and told them to get me a bird with good instrumentation. My plan was to fly instruments above the mountains to the pickup site and then let down into the mountain visually using flares. We would use our FM homing device to find the patients. Once we had the patients on board, I would do a steep instrument takeoff into the clouds and weather above the mountains, fly out over the coast and let down over the water near the lights of Chu Lai. That's what I did, four times. I used 3 copilots that night but got all the patients out.

We used this technique on other occasions and never failed to get the patients. We now had solutions to the night weather problem. As I said, we had 23 Purple Heart medals, but we never lost an aircraft or a crew member due to the night or the weather. This was despite the fact that we flew thousands of night and weather missions, had some 117 of our aircraft damaged by enemy fire each month and carried over 20,000 patients in 10 months. In the three months following our tour, the same small unit had 5 crew members killed. God had certainly watched over us.

I received the Distinguished Service Cross for the night flare mission and numerous other awards for my flying in Vietnam. As a result, one encyclopedia lists me as the war's top helicopter pilot. The truth is that I was an average pilot who came within an eyelash of busting out of flight school. My instructor pilot said I was dangerous, and there are to this day some of my copilots who will swear I can't read a map. There is no way I could have flown the missions

I flew on my own. I will not say that God was my copilot because I could not have made it without the copilots I had. For my part, I had a strong faith that shielded me from fear, and I cared about the troops. But it was God who showed me the way, who was my Light as I stumbled through the darkness and the fog and the clouds of my doubts.

—*Pat Brady*

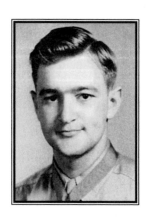

Charles H. Coolidge
U.S. Army • WWII

"My creed and formula for successful living is simple. It sustained me through World War II: Trust not in thine own self but put your faith in Almighty God, and He will see you through. I had this brought home to me in vivid fashion on Hill 623 in southern France during WWII. Although faced with possible annihilation by an enemy force of greater numbers, my small body of brave soldiers overcame these overwhelming odds.

"Hill 623 in southern France will remain steadfast in my memory. The action that occurred there resulted in my being awarded the Medal of Honor, which is our country's highest military decoration. But I must be quick to state that the act that took place on a hill at Calvary far exceeds any victory that man can conceive. It was there that the Lord laid down His life for all who would believe and accept His gift of grace. Through His resurrection, victory over Satan was wrought and the plan of salvation became a living truth.

"For young people, I recommend that they set their priorities straight. Put God first in all things, and the remaining issues will fall in line. Simply conduct oneself in such a manner that if Christ should suddenly appear, personal behavior would prove no embarrassment to Him or to oneself. Be honest in all dealings with other people and share the love of Christ with whomever you find oppressed or despondent. And, finally, to thine own self be true lest you prove false to your fellow men. This is something that has sustained me through the trials of battle and the troublesome encounters of civilian life."

————•••••————

Rank and organization
Technical Sergeant, U.S. Army, Company M,
141st Infantry, 36th Infantry Division.
Place and date
East of Belmont sur Buttant, France, 24-27 October 1944.

CITATION
Leading a section of heavy machineguns supported by 1 platoon of Company K, he took a position near Hill 623, east of Belmont sur Buttant, France, on 24 October 1944, with the mission of covering the right flank of the 3d Battalion and supporting its action. T/Sgt. Coolidge went forward with a sergeant of Company K to reconnoiter positions for coordinating the fires of the light and heavy machine guns.

They ran into an enemy force in the woods estimated to be an infantry company. T/Sgt. Coolidge, attempting to bluff the Germans by a show of assurance and boldness, called upon them to surrender, whereupon the enemy opened fire. With his carbine, T/Sgt. Coolidge wounded two of them. There being no officer present with the force, T/Sgt. Coolidge at once assumed command. Many of the men were replacements recently arrived; this was their first experience under fire. T/Sgt. Coolidge, unmindful of the enemy fire delivered at close range, walked along the position, calming and encouraging his men and directing their fire. The attack was thrown back.

Through 25 and 26 October, the enemy launched repeated attacks against the position of this combat group, but each was repulsed due to T/Sgt. Coolidge's able leadership. On 27 October, German infantry, supported by 2 tanks, made a determined attack on the position. The area was swept by enemy small arms, machinegun, and tank fire. T/Sgt. Coolidge armed himself with a bazooka and advanced to within 25 yards of the tanks. His bazooka failed to function and he threw it aside. Securing all the hand grenades he could carry, he crawled forward and inflicted heavy casualties on the advancing enemy. Finally it became apparent that the enemy, in greatly superior force, supported by tanks, would overrun the position. T/Sgt. Coolidge, displaying great coolness and courage, directed and conducted an orderly withdrawal, being himself the last to leave the position.

As a result of T/Sgt. Coolidge's heroic and superior leadership, the mission of this combat group was accomplished throughout four days of continuous fighting against numerically superior enemy troops in rain and cold and amid dense woods.

SHADOW OF DEATH – FEAR NOT

Ever since the fall of Adam, man has struggled to live in peace on this planet. The entry of Satan has wrought havoc on men and nations alike. Fierce battles have been fought to prevent world domination by satanic powers. Unfortunately, man has not solved this ongoing dilemma, and the threat of war still exists.

As I survey my military combat experience during World War II, I am confident that it was my strong Christian faith that sustained me during fierce battles. I held to the firm belief to trust not in thine ownself, but place your faith in Almighty God and He will see you through. On Hill 623 in southern France during that global war, although faced with possible annihilation by a numerically superior enemy force, I did not fear the enemy who sought to overwhelm me on the field of battle.

Never did personal fear enter the situation. I kept remembering the words of my pastor back home. When I was a boy, he would recite the Bible story of David and Goliath and others who faced tremendous odds. I knew that same supernatural power was available to those who believed and remained faithful to God's commands. These memories helped to sustain me.

My sense of security was derived from the Christian training afforded me by my parents. Blessed with a godly mother who served as a Sunday School superintendent and by a devout father who planted country churches and preached at missions stations, I possessed a protective blanket from caring parents whose chief interest was serving the Lord. It naturally followed that I would be the beneficiary of their petitioning prayers, particularly during my military service.

I served twenty months in combat with 133 consecutive days of contact with the enemy (a World War II record). It is a miracle of God's grace and care that I received no wounds or injuries and returned home safely after front-line fighting through North Africa, Italy, France, Germany, and Austria. I give God the praise and the glory for His protection.

The Lord laid down His life for all who would believe and accept His gift of grace. Through His resurrection, victory over Satan was won and the plan of salvation became a living truth. That is victory in its highest form.

—*Charles Coolidge*

Desmond T. Doss
U.S. Army WWII

"I would like to share my godly mother's advice: Live by the Golden Rule and do unto others as you would have them do unto you. Study the Bible daily, for it is God's love letter to us letting us know right from wrong; it is our road map to heaven. He has not asked us to give up anything good, only that which is not good enough for life eternal with Him and our loved ones. Eye hath not seen nor ear heard, neither hath it entered into the heart of man the wonderful things He has gone to prepare for us who love Him and keep His holy law. If we miss heaven, we have missed everything."

Rank and organization
Private First Class, U.S. Army, Medical Detachment,
307th Infantry, 77th Infantry Division.
Place and date
Near Urasoe Mura, Okinawa, Ryukyu Islands, 4/29–5/21/45.

CITATION

He was a company aid man when the 1st Battalion assaulted a jagged escarpment 400 feet high. As our troops gained the summit, a heavy concentration of artillery, mortar and machinegun fire crashed into them, inflicting approximately 75 casualties and driving the others back. Pfc. Doss refused to seek cover and remained in the fire-swept area with the many stricken, carrying them one by one to the edge of the escarpment and there lowering them on a rope-supported litter down the face of a cliff to friendly hands.

On 2 May, he exposed himself to heavy rifle and mortar fire in rescuing a wounded man 200 yards forward of the lines on the same escarpment; and two days later he treated four men who had been cut down while assaulting a strongly defended cave, advancing through a shower of grenades to within eight yards of enemy forces in a cave's mouth, where he dressed his comrades' wounds before making four separate trips under fire to evacuate them to safety.

On 5 May, he unhesitatingly braved enemy shelling and small arms fire to assist an artillery officer. He applied bandages, moved his patient to a spot that offered protection from small arms fire and, while artillery and mortar shells fell close by, painstakingly administered plasma. Later that day, when an American was severely wounded by fire from a cave, Pfc. Doss crawled to him where he had fallen 25 feet from the enemy position, rendered aid, and carried him 100 yards to safety while continually exposed to enemy fire.

On 21 May, in a night attack on high ground near Shuri, he remained in exposed territory while the rest of his company took cover, fearlessly risking the chance that he would be mistaken for an infiltrating Japanese and giving aid to the injured until he was himself seriously wounded in the legs by the explosion of a grenade. Rather than call another aid man from cover, he cared for his own injuries and waited five hours before litter bearers reached him and started carrying him to cover. The trio was caught in an enemy tank attack and Pfc. Doss, seeing a more critically wounded man nearby, crawled off the litter and directed the bearers to give their first attention to the other man. Awaiting the litter bearers' return, he was again struck, this time suffering a compound fracture of one arm. With magnificent fortitude, he bound a rifle stock to his shattered arm as a splint and then crawled 300 yards over rough terrain to the aid station.

Through his outstanding bravery and unflinching determination in the face of desperately dangerous conditions, Pfc. Doss saved the lives of many soldiers. His name became a symbol throughout the 77th Infantry Division for outstanding gallantry far above and beyond the call of duty.

MIRACLE DAY

On the island of Okinawa in the Pacific is a big hill called the Maeda Escarpment. It is a hill that goes up gradually on one side, levels off on top and then drops off 400 feet to the valley below. During World War II, the American army was in the valley below the 400 foot drop off. It wasn't easy to get up the cliff the first 365 feet, but it was possible. But the last 35 feet was straight up and jutted out about five feet at the top.

I was a medic in B company attached to the 307th regiment of the 77th infantry division, the Statue of Liberty Division. We had fought on top of the escarpment for a number of days without much progress being made. The escarpment was honeycombed with caves and tunnels. The Japanese put ladders from one cave or tunnel to another on the inside of the escarpment. On top were foxholes that looked like natural terrain, making it easy for them to shoot Americans who didn't even know they were there.

As we prepared to go up on top of the escarpment again this particular day, I went to Lieutenant Gornto and suggested, "I believe prayer is the best life-saver there is." Immediately he called our group together and said, "Gather round, fellows. Doss wants to pray for us."

Now that was not what I had in mind. I just wanted to remind the men that none of us was sure of a return down the escarpment because we knew how fierce the fighting was, and that each man should pray for himself. But after the lieutenant said that, I did pray. I prayed that God would be with the lieutenant and help him to give us the correct orders as our lives were in his hands and help each one of us to take all the safety precautions necessary so that we could all come back alive.

With that we started up the escarpment and immediately got pinned down and thought we couldn't move. Shortly a message came through headquarters asking what our losses were. I answered, "None so far."

Again a message came through. "Company A who is fighting

on your left, has been so badly shot up, they can't do any more. Company B will have to take the whole escarpment by yourselves." How would you like to get orders like that? Uncle Sam has to sacrifice lives to take important objectives, and the Maeda Escarpment was a very important objective.

So we started to move forward. As I remember, Company B started to take enemy positions one at a time until we had taken eight or nine Japanese positions. The amazing part of it was that not a single man from Company B was killed, and only one man was slightly wounded by a rock that hit his hand. That was one day that I, as a medic, didn't have much to do.

It was such an amazing happening that word began to get around to various companies, to headquarters, and even back to the States. The men of Company B were asked, "How did you manage to do that?" Their answer, "Due to Doss' prayer." They recognized that God had cared for them in a very special way because of the prayer of protection.

The next day we were to go up on the escarpment again. We figured the work was done and this was just a mop-up job. I didn't pray and I doubt if anyone else did either. That day everything went wrong. The men would throw grenades and other high explosives, and the Japanese would pull the fuses before they went off. A number of my men were wounded and needed help. Four men were together in a forward position. One of them tried to throw a grenade. It went off prematurely and he lost his hand. The other three were also wounded. I went to them, did a little first aid and then carried them back one-by-one to the edge of the escarpment.

There was one Japanese foxhole that was giving us trouble. In spite of all the ammunition our men directed into the foxhole, it was still active and in Japanese hands. Finally several of the men opened cans of high octane gasoline and threw the cans and the gas into the foxhole. I understand a lieutenant threw a white phosphorous grenade into the gasoline. The resulting explosion was much more than expected. All of the ammunition the men had thrown into the foxhole exploded; probably the Japanese ammunition dump down below went off too.

What happened next was also unexpected. The Japanese evidently figured it was now or never, and they came at us from all sides. The command was given to retreat. Many of our men were wounded and remained on top of the escarpment. They were my men and I felt I could not leave them. I started to pull them to the edge, and one-by-one I began to let them down using a double bowline knot that I had worked with one time while still in the states. It made two loops that could be pulled over the feet and up the legs of the wounded soldiers. Then I would tie another bowline knot around their chest and let them down the first 35 feet to where they could be carried to the aid station. The Lord even provided a tree stump that I could wind rope around and let them down easy.

I kept praying, "Lord, help me get one more." The Lord answered my prayer. I was able to get all the men down that day. The army said it was 100, but I told them it couldn't be more than 50. So my citation for the Medal of Honor says 75.

On October 12th, 1945, President Truman presented me with the Congressional Medal of Honor. I believe that I received the Medal of Honor because I remembered to keep the Golden Rule as stated in Matthew 7:12, "Therefore all things whatsoever ye would that men should do to you, do ye even so to them."

—*Desmond T. Doss*

Walter D. Ehlers
U.S. Army • WWII

"When I enlisted in the United States Army, I had to get my dad's and mother's signatures. My dad had agreed to sign. My mother said, with tears in her eyes, 'I will sign if you promise to be a Christian soldier.' I assured her I would do my best. It wasn't easy being a Christian soldier, but each time I was tempted, I would see the tears in my mother's eyes and I would remember my promise.

"I also would realize I had made a commitment to God. I had no intention of dishonoring my mother and, above all, God. My faith in God, my fellow men, and myself, made the difference. This is why I am a survivor of the war. In order to have faith in yourself, you must arm yourself with complete knowledge of your job. Requirements include honesty, compassion, courage, education, faith, and commitment. I am not a saint, but my faith and determination to do my best worked for me."

Rank and organization
Staff Sergeant, U.S. Army, 18th Infantry, 1st Infantry Division.
Place and date
Near Goville, France, 9-10 June 1944.

CITATION

For conspicuous gallantry and intrepidity at the risk of his life above and beyond the call of duty on 9-10 June 1944, near Goville, France.

S/Sgt. Ehlers, always acting as the spearhead of the attack, repeatedly led his men against heavily defended enemy strong points exposing himself to deadly hostile fire whenever the situation required heroic and courageous leadership. Without waiting for an order, S/Sgt. Ehlers, far ahead of his men, led his squad against a strongly defended enemy strong point, personally killing 4 of an enemy patrol who attacked him en route. Then crawling forward under withering machinegun fire, he pounced upon the guncrew and put it out of action. Turning his attention to 2 mortars protected by the crossfire of 2 machineguns, S/Sgt. Ehlers led his men through this hail of bullets to kill or put to flight the enemy of the mortar section, killing 3 men himself. After mopping up the mortar positions, he again advanced on a machinegun, his progress effectively covered by his squad. When he was almost on top of the gun, he leaped to his feet and, although greatly outnumbered, he knocked out the position single-handed.

The next day, having advanced deep into enemy territory, the platoon of which S/Sgt. Ehlers was a member, finding itself in an untenable position as the enemy brought increased mortar, machinegun, and small arms fire to bear on it, was ordered to withdraw. S/Sgt. Ehlers, after his squad had covered the withdrawal of the remainder of the platoon, stood up and by continuous fire at the semicircle of enemy placements, diverted the bulk of the heavy hostile fire on himself, thus permitting the members of his own squad to withdraw. At this point, though wounded himself, he carried his wounded automatic rifleman to safety and then returned fearlessly over the shell-swept field to retrieve the automatic rifle which he was unable to carry previously. After having his wound treated, he refused to be evacuated, and returned to lead his squad.

The intrepid leadership, indomitable courage, and fearless aggressiveness displayed by S/Sgt. Ehlers in the face of overwhelming enemy forces serve as an inspiration to others.

⬥••◦••⬥

THE PRAYERS OF A MOTHER

I grew up on a farm near Manhattan, Kansas. My oldest brother, Roland, and I both enlisted at the same time and began our training at Fort Lewis, Washington. When we found out we were going to North Africa, we were in the same Infantry company. We landed at Casablanca and were together during the North Africa campaign, and we were together again in Sicily. Roland was wounded in Sicily and was sent back to Africa to recover, but we were together again in England before the Normandy Invasion on D-Day. Because of the danger, our company Commander decided to put us in different companies prior to the invasion.

On D-Day, my landing craft dropped us off in water so deep that it was over our heads. When we finally made it to the beach, the men wanted to lie down. I told them we had to get off the beach or we would all be killed. We made our way up a steep hill and knocked out a bunker. This allowed us to get off the beach. Over the next few days I tried to find out about Roland, but he was declared Missing-In-Action. It was over a month before I finally received the news that he had been killed on the beach when his landing craft was hit by mortar or artillery fire.

Within a few days, my squad was involved in fierce fighting. It was because of this action that the men in my squad requested that I receive the Medal of Honor. During the firefight, I was wounded by an enemy sniper. The bullet struck me in the ribs and went around to my back and into my backpack. The bullet tore through the pack and struck the edge of my mother's picture.

During the war I carried and read my pocket New Testament that included the Psalms. I found great comfort in reading the twenty-third Psalm and the Lord's Prayer. I also found great comfort knowing that my family, and especially my mother, were praying for me. In every letter I received from my mother, she told me she was praying for me and for my two brothers. She had three sons in the war.

I guess my New Testament must have been lost when I was wounded. About ten years after the war, it arrived in the mail. A German lady sent it to my mother because her name and address were written in the front pages of the Bible. Apparently the woman's children found the Bible under some rocks behind their home. The lady, not knowing if I survived the war, said she wanted to send the Bible, hoping that it would comfort my mother. Mom was thrilled to receive it, but she was just as excited to realize that it was worn from my reading it during the war. She realized that I had tried to be a Christian soldier. My mother was an inspiration to me and to our family. Where would we be without mothers that pray for us?

—*Walter Ehlers*

Brigadier General Joseph Foss
U.S. Marine Corps, U.S. Air Force Reserve
(Ret.) USMC • WWII

"During World War II, God saved me over and over and over again. I have no excuse for being here. I often say that God was saving me for later duty. Bible study and sharing my faith occupy much of my time. I frequently speak to different groups and am often asked the question, 'Of all the honors and awards that you have received, what do you consider the most important, number one?' I am able to look them in the eye and say, 'The day that I invited Jesus Christ into my life as my Lord and Savior is number one.'"

Rank and organization
Captain, U.S. Marine Corps Reserve,
Marine Fighting Squadron 121, 1st Marine Aircraft Wing.
Place and date
Over Guadalcanal, 9 October to 19 November 1942,
15 and 23 January 1943.

CITATION

For outstanding heroism and courage above and beyond the call of duty as executive officer of Marine Fighting Squadron 121, 1st Marine Aircraft Wing, at Guadalcanal. Engaging in almost daily combat with the enemy from 9 October to 19 November 1942, Capt. Foss personally shot down 23 Japanese planes and damaged others so severely that their destruction was extremely probable.

In addition, during this period, he successfully led a large number of escort missions, skillfully covering reconnaissance, bombing, and photographic planes as well as surface craft. On 15 January 1943, he added 3 more enemy planes to his already brilliant successes for a record of aerial combat achievement unsurpassed in this war. Boldly searching out an approaching enemy force on 25 January, Capt. Foss led his 8 F-4F Marine planes and 4 Army P-38s into action and, undaunted by tremendously superior numbers, intercepted and struck with such force that 4 Japanese fighters were shot down and the bombers were turned back without releasing a single bomb.

His remarkable flying skill, inspiring leadership, and indomitable fighting spirit were distinctive factors in the defense of strategic American positions on Guadalcanal.

SAVED FOR LATER DUTY

It was November of 1943 and I was about to experience one of the most frightening experiences of my life. While on a mission, we spotted a Japanese flotilla with air cover from six float Zeros, equipped with pontoons for water takeoffs. We were able to shoot down the six Zeros but not without the loss of one of our planes and pilot.

As we prepared to attack the Japanese ships, I spotted another Japanese plane. I flew upward to get above the bogey. When he emerged from the cloud, I made a diving run toward the plane. I quickly realized that I had overestimated my adversary. The plane was not the faster and nimbler Zero but was a slower scout plane with a rear gunner. I dove too fast and had to roll on my side to avoid crashing into the rear of the plane. The pilot rolled as well, giving his tail gunner a perfect shot at me, at point blank range. The shells pierced the left side of my engine cowling and shattered the canopy on the side of my plane just a few inches from my face. Initially it appeared that there was no serious damage, but because of the damage to my plane, I was unable to dive and I watched the planes of VMF-121 attack the Japanese ships. With a second pass, I was able to shoot down the scout plane and then came upon a second scout plane that I was also able to bring down—my eighteenth and nineteenth victory in air combat.

As I looked for the rest of my flight, I saw them off in the distance over a mile away flying to get out of range of the ship's gun to regroup and head back to the base. I tried to call the departing planes but couldn't raise anyone. Apparently the radio was dead, probably one of the Japanese shells had damaged the aerial. As the engine of the plane started to miss and backfire puffing out white smoke, I headed for the rendezvous point. I had to throttle back repeatedly to prevent the engine from conking out. At this point I was getting nervous. The others had long since regrouped and headed back. I was beginning to lose altitude when I ran into rain-squalls and heavy clouds.

Breaking out of the clouds, I could make out two islands and headed toward them. I mistook them for the gateway to Guadalcanal. After awhile the engine stops got closer than the starts, and I realized that I wasn't going to make it back to Henderson Field. Another squall appeared dead ahead and I flew to circumvent it. When I came abreast of the storm, the engine stopped cold. I knew that if I landed in the water, my chances of being spotted were minimal, if not nonexistent. I lamented the fact that I had never learned to swim. I spotted an island and I set my glide path for it. I figured that I had plenty of altitude to make the distance. I planned to ditch the plane directly offshore and paddle to land with the aid of my Mae West. Believing that I might find a sandy beach to land on, I circled over the deserted shoreline. I realized that I miscalculated: The maneuver cost me the needed altitude.

When I circled back out to sea, I realized that I was going down in the water about five miles from land. As the plane descended and the water rose to meet me, I pulled the nose of the plane up, hoping to skip the plane along the surface of the water. The tail hit the water and bounced up above the front of the plane. When I hit the water a second time, I nosed into the Pacific like a torpedo from a dive-bomber. The heavily armored plane sank almost immediately. I found myself in utter darkness with water gushing into the cockpit. Trapped in the plane, I forced myself to act. As water filled the cockpit, I felt for the latches that held the canopy, unfastened them, and pushed it open with all my strength. I fought to maintain consciousness, but momentarily blacked out and sucked in the brackish sea water. Just as the story goes, my whole life passed before my eyes. Forcing myself to action was agony, and I restrained my gagging through sheer force of will. Reaching down I unhooked my leg straps, swallowing more sea water in the process.

No longer locked in the plane, I was pulled upward toward the surface by the force of the current streaming past the rapidly sinking Wildcat. At the same time, my left foot caught and wedged under the cockpit seat, trapping me and holding me fast as the Wildcat continued its descent into the deep. I pulled my way, hand over hand, toward my captured foot. I used the last of my strength to free myself, and I felt the crushing pressure of the cold water as I shot upward. My need for air was pure pain. When I hit the surface, I adjusted the straps of my Mae West and all of a sudden I was floating.

I realized the odds of making it to the island were slim, between the storm, the rapidly approaching darkness, and the current that seemed to be carrying me out to sea. To make matters worse, a short distance away something caught my eye, "Shark fins!" I believe I even yelled it out loud! I thought, "What a way to go. After all I've been through, I'm going to check out as a hunk of shark bait." Trying to swim became doubly fearful. Every time I reached an arm out to paddle, I was afraid I'd draw back a stub. I started praying harder than I'd ever prayed in my life. I confessed every sin I could remember and kept praying, "God help me." I never felt more alone or helpless. I drifted for four or five hours. I was growing weaker as I struggled against the sea. Through the black of the night I heard something. Voices! I turned my head in the direction of the sounds. Canoe paddles? "Japs!" I thought. "They saw me go down." I stopped swimming and floated silently. The splashing of the oars grew louder. Two boats were traveling toward me; I heard men speaking but could not make out the mumbled conversations. The searchers combed the waters, back and forth. Finally someone yelled, "Let's look over 'ere." It was an Australian accent and the most welcome sound I'd ever heard. "Hey!" I yelled. "Over here!" A hand reached out of the darkness and pulled me into the outrigger. It was the hand of Father Dan Stuyvenberg, a Catholic priest. As the men talked, they told me that the piece of land that I'd been swimming toward was populated with man-eating crocodiles.

Today I realize that God saved me over and over and over. I have no excuse for being in the world today except that the Lord was saving me for another battle. I could have been killed by the gunfire that brought my plane down. I could have died in the crash landing, could have drowned, could have been killed by sharks or man-eating crocodiles or captured and killed by the Japanese, but God saved me.

Adapted from *A PROUD AMERICAN, The Autobiography of Joe Foss*, Pocket Books.

Rodolfo "Rudy" Hernandez
U.S. Army • Korea

"I believe in God Almighty. There were times in my life that God meant more to me than anyone else. He forgives us of sin, gives us abundant life, and is full of mercy.

"I was pleased to fight for my country not only because I was born in the United States, but because I believe it is the land of promise and hope.

"Finally, I love the flag. I hold it in respect."

Rank and organization
Corporal, U.S. Army, Company G,
187th Airborne Regimental Combat Team.
Place and date
Near Wontong-ni, Korea, 31 May 1951.

CITATION

Cpl. Hernandez, a member of Company G, distinguished himself by conspicuous gallantry and intrepidity above and beyond the call of duty in action against the enemy.

His platoon, in defensive positions on Hill 420, came under ruthless attack by a numerically superior and fanatical hostile force, accompanied by heavy artillery, mortar, and machine gun fire which inflicted numerous casualties on the platoon. His comrades were forced to withdraw due to lack of ammunition but Cpl. Hernandez, although wounded in an exchange of grenades, continued to deliver deadly fire into the ranks of the onrushing assailants until a ruptured cartridge rendered his rifle inoperative. Immediately leaving his position, Cpl. Hernandez rushed the enemy armed only with rifle and bayonet. Fearlessly engaging the foe, he killed 6 of the enemy before falling unconscious from grenade, bayonet, and bullet wounds, but his heroic action momentarily halted the enemy advance and enabled his unit to counterattack and retake the lost ground.

The indomitable fighting spirit, outstanding courage, and tenacious devotion to duty clearly demonstrated by Cpl. Hernandez reflect the highest credit upon himself, the infantry, and the U.S. Army.

I AM NOT ASHAMED

I am proud to be a Medal of Honor recipient. I am also proud of my Hispanic heritage, of being an American, and of being an Army paratrooper. I carry a business card with the image of the Medal of Honor and my name on the front of the card. When you turn the card over, you will read the words, "I am not ashamed of the gospel of Jesus Christ." Faith in God is an important part of my life. I have a deep faith in God because He has been so good to me.

During the Korean War, I was an Army Infantryman with the 187th Regimental Combat Team, frequently referred to as the RAAKASANS. I was already an experienced combat veteran by February 1951. During one battle, I changed places with my friend, and he was killed almost immediately. I realized that bullet was meant for me.

On the 31st of May, 1951, my platoon came under a ruthless attack by a numerically superior enemy force. We were near Wontong-ni, Korea on Hill 420. The initial attack was from heavy artillery, mortar, and machine-gun fire and was followed by an over-whelming number of enemy soldiers.

Many of the men in the platoon were wounded, and the decision was made to withdraw. I remained to cover the withdrawal even though I was wounded by artillery shrapnel. While I was firing my rifle, one of the cartridges in my weapon ruptured and rendered the rifle inoperable. I placed the bayonet on my rifle and rushed toward the enemy. I made the decision to counter-attack in an effort to save the lives of my comrades.

During the counter-attack, I was severely wounded by artillery shrapnel from an air-burst and rifle fire, and I was bayoneted twice. But my efforts halted their assault, which allowed my unit to counterattack and retake our position. I was wounded so severely that I was placed in a body bag because everyone assumed that I was dead. Someone finally realized that I was still alive when they saw my hand move.

The artillery shrapnel tore my helmet from my head and a large part of my skull and a part of my brain was severely injured. I was paralyzed, unconscious, and in a coma for a month. When I finally regained consciousness, I had to relearn how to swallow, eat, feed myself, walk, and speak. I was transferred to Letterman Army Hospital in San Francisco where surgeons tried to repair the damage to my skull, face, arm, and leg. A large part of my skull had been destroyed, and the surgeons performed experimental surgery to close the large defect in my skull. Months passed before I was able to speak a single word.

It took twelve years for me to recover from the massive injuries that I sustained. I underwent multiple surgeries for five years and spent the next eight years working to regain control of my body. I still do not have complete use of my right arm and hand, but I learned to write and do most things with my left hand.

After all I have been through, I came to the conclusion that only by the grace of God and His mercy am I alive today. It gives me great joy to be able to say and to share with others that "I am not ashamed of the gospel of Jesus Christ."

—*Rodolfo "Rudy" Hernandez*

Robert D. Maxwell
U.S. Army • WWII

"Much of our success in life is determined by how we handle our anxieties and fears of the unknown future. Because of fear, we may be hesitant to step out into avenues of opportunity. Our anxieties may cause us to miss much of life's good things.

"We can draw consolation from two teachings of Jesus: 1) Let Him handle anxieties (Matt. 6:25-34); and 2) Fear can be displaced by love (1 John 4:17-18). When we have the love that comes from God, we can overcome the anxieties that accompany very frightening situations. Our own concern for self-preservation, though very important to us, is less than our concern for others we love. This is why people often risk their life to save others (John 15:13)."

Rank and organization
Technician Fifth Grade, U.S. Army,
7th Infantry, 3d Infantry Division.
Place and date
Near Besancon, France, 7 September 1944.

CITATION
For conspicuous gallantry and intrepidity at risk of life above and beyond the call of duty on 7 September 1944, near Besancon, France.

Technician 5th Grade Maxwell and 3 other soldiers, armed only with .45 caliber automatic pistols, defended the battalion observation post against an overwhelming onslaught by enemy infantrymen in approximately platoon strength, supported by 20mm. flak and machinegun fire, who had infiltrated through the battalion's forward companies and were attacking the observation post with machinegun, machine pistol, and grenade fire at ranges as close as 10 yards. Despite a hail of fire from automatic weapons and grenade launchers, Technician 5th Grade Maxwell aggressively fought off advancing enemy elements and, by his calmness, tenacity, and fortitude, inspired his fellows to continue the unequal struggle. When an enemy hand grenade was thrown in the midst of his squad, Technician 5th Grade Maxwell unhesitatingly hurled himself squarely upon it, using his blanket and his unprotected body to absorb the full force of the explosion.

This act of instantaneous heroism permanently maimed Technician 5th Grade Maxwell, but saved the lives of his comrades in arms and facilitated maintenance of vital military communications during the temporary withdrawal of the battalion's forward headquarters.

THE SHIELD OF FAITH

I believe that faith is the most important aspect of humanity. "Faith is being sure of what we hope for and certain of what we do not see" (Hebrews 11:1 NIV). It takes faith in a higher authority than ourselves for progress to take place in our lives. Many, if not most, of America's great leaders expressed a trust in God as an influence on their success. Those gallant men who officiated at the birth of our nation trusted and had a faith in God as the Higher Power to watch over the struggling colonies. We see the results of their faith and works and those of many great leaders throughout the centuries, which culminated in the development of this great nation that has always offered liberty to the world's oppressed. Since our beginning, we have fought wars endeavoring to maintain that liberty throughout the free world.

Without faith, the fighting forces of our nation cannot perform their duty. They must trust in the authority above them, from the commander-in-chief down to their squad leader. For example, when danger threatens the very existence of the combat soldier, he must rely on his training, experience, fellow soldiers, and that Higher Power—God—to survive. Every combat veteran can say, "I know, I've been there."

Faith, even if just newly found, has the ability to change lives. I met a retired veteran a few years ago who told me his story. His military career included a life of alcohol abuse. Over time he became an alcoholic, a disease that is permanent and unrelenting. On December 7, 1976, he "kicked the habit" and joined with others who had a similar problem and started in the Alcoholic's Anonymous program. It's hard for anyone with a "macho" image, who is self-sufficient and also a determined person, to believe in any force greater than himself. The man and his wife were invited to attend church. While visiting with a few of the men from the congregation, he met three veterans in the parking lot.

One of these veterans had served as a Marine Raider in World War II and also had survived the desperate fighting and winter at the Chosin Reservoir in Korea. The former Marine was the father of the pastor of the church. Another of the veterans was a former Army Air Corps B-17 radio operator and upper turret gunner. This veteran's plane had been shot down over Germany. He was seriously injured when he made a parachute landing on the concrete road of a small German town. He spent the remainder of the war as a POW in Stalag 17. The other veteran had received the Medal of Honor. His infantry career ended with the blast from a German grenade in France.

After meeting and visiting these veterans, he realized that these men were for real. As a result, he and his wife were immersed in Christian love. Our friendship continued over the years. Our "alcoholic" friend had finally found something in which to believe. He found the power that would help him overcome and control the craving monster that had dominated his life. He no longer had to face his problem alone.

He now had the assurance that this new life included faith in a Mediator who would intercede with God about his requests and needs. Fortunately this experience, this faith, is available to all of us.

—*Robert Maxwell*

Colonel Mitchell Paige
U.S. Marine Corps (Ret.) WWII

"My parents and teachers instilled in me a devout love of God, family, and country. When I left home after high school to enlist in the Marines, my God-fearing mother admonished me to 'Just trust in God always.' Six years later, right after the fierce battle on Guadalcanal, I emptied the contents of my combat pack, and because of my burned hands, I gingerly picked up my pocket New Testament which included the Psalms and Proverbs. The page providentially opened to Proverbs 3:5-6: 'Trust in the Lord with all your heart, and lean not on your own understanding. In all your ways acknowledge Him and He will direct your paths.'

"My greatest earthly honor was being awarded the Congressional Medal of Honor. My highest honor—bar none—is, as a sinner, to know Jesus Christ as my Lord and Savior and through Him to know the peace of heart that passes all human understanding.

I believe any American with firm moral convictions and courage to defend them at any cost is able to defend himself and maintain his integrity. Valor and patriotism, virtues of the highest order, are part of our beliefs which we must never forget. Since its birth in 1776, our great nation has proudly proclaimed the cherished slogan, 'IN GOD WE TRUST.' Someone once said, 'The evidence of God's presence far outweighs the proof of His absence.'"

———◆◆◆◆———

Rank and organization
Platoon Sergeant, U.S. Marine Corps.
Place and date
Solomon Islands, 26 October 1942

CITATION

For extraordinary heroism and conspicuous gallantry in action above and beyond the call of duty while serving with a company of Marines in combat against enemy Japanese forces in the Solomon Islands on 26 October 1942.

When the enemy broke through the line directly in front of his position, P/Sgt. Paige, commanding a machinegun section with fearless determination, continued to direct the fire of his gunners until all his men were either killed or wounded. Alone, against the deadly hail of Japanese shells, he fought with his gun and when it was destroyed, took over another, moving from gun to gun, never ceasing his withering fire against the advancing hordes until reinforcements finally arrived. Then, forming a new line, he dauntlessly and aggressively led a bayonet charge, driving the enemy back and preventing a breakthrough in our lines.

His great personal valor and unyielding devotion to duty were in keeping with the highest traditions of the U.S. Naval Service.

TRUST IN THE LORD

When I left home to enlist in the Marine Corps, my mother told me, "All I want you to do is trust in the Lord; don't try to figure out everything by yourself, and God will show you the way." I joined the Marines in 1936 after I finished high school. During the battle of Guadalcanal, I was a platoon Sergeant in H Company, 2nd Battalion, 7th Regiment, 1st Marines. Following the initial landing on Guadalcanal, the Marines captured the Japanese airfield and named it Henderson Field.

On October 26th, 1942, I was involved in the crucial battle that prevented the enemy from over-running and recapturing Henderson Field. My 33-man platoon was positioned on a ridge within clear observation of the Japanese and Japanese artillery fire. Throughout the day of October 25th, we waited with great anticipation for night to fall. We knew the enemy was aware of our position. Marine patrols had reported that a large body of enemy troops was moving toward our position. Two battalions of the Japanese 124th Infantry Regiment and one Battalion of the 4th Infantry— comprised of about 2,500 to 3,000 enemy soldiers—were moving into position to assault the ridge.

Although the platoon was under strength, we knew we had to hold the ridge at all costs. I moved up and down the line to encourage every Marine and to tell them to hold their fire until the enemy could be seen clearly. Very early in the morning on the 26th of October, we began to see movement below us. As the battle erupted, the enemy advanced to the ridge and our position. The battle became a life and death struggle all along the ridge. After the first wave, a second wave came and the enemy was close to controlling the ridge. Every member of my platoon was either killed or wounded. It was a living hell. I continued to fire my machine gun until the barrel began to steam. In front of me, there was a large pile of dead Japanese soldiers. I ran along the ridge from gun to gun trying to keep them firing, but at each emplacement, I found only dead bodies.

Once when I was running between the gun positions, an enemy soldier rushed at me and with a thrust of his bayonet cut the fingers of my hand. I pushed his rifle aside and using my K-Bar knife, I killed the enemy soldier. A few minutes later, I found myself racing an enemy soldier to one of the gun emplacements. I got there first, but I discovered that the weapon was not loaded. As I tried desperately to pull the bolt back on the machine gun, a strange feeling came over me. I was unable to lean forward; it was like my body was in a vise. Even with that, I felt relaxed and had no fear. All of a sudden, I felt a release from the vise-like hold, and I fell forward over the gun. At the exact moment that this was happening, the enemy soldier had fired his full 30-round magazine at me. I felt the heat and the blast of those bullets pass close to my face and chin. Had I been able to lean forward and pull the bolt back on the machine gun, the bullets would have hit me in the head. I realized I had been spared and protected by an invisible shield.

As dawn broke on the 26th of October, the platoon, now only 26 men, rallied to charge and counterattack. As we ran toward the enemy, I was carrying a red-hot machine gun cradled across my bare arms and hands. With the counterattack, the remaining enemy withdrew. Returning to my gun position, I began to empty the contents of my combat pack to find my Bible. Because my hands were burned by the hot metal barrel of the machine gun, I was unable to hold the Bible. It fell to the ground and it opened to the third chapter of Proverbs. It opened to the chapter and verse given as an admonition from my mother when I left home in 1936. "Trust in the Lord with all your heart and lean not to your own understanding. In all your ways acknowledge Him and He will direct your path." Another Marine ran up to me. He told me later that I was standing there talking to myself, saying, "Mom, Mom." I know the greatest earthly honor that can be given to an American fighting man is the Medal of Honor. But my highest honor, bar none, is to know Jesus Christ as my Lord and Savior.

—*Mitchell Paige*

Colonel Leo K. Thorsness
U.S. Air Force (Ret.) • Vietnam

"While a POW in Hanoi for six years, I put into conscious thinking a 'plan for life.' My formula is very basic. It is this: Life = Goals + Commitments + Plans. My definition of life is: living a full, productive Christian life.

"GOALS: Goals take a lot of cerebration—a lot of deep thinking. I'm talking about two or three major goals in life. For most, that includes the spiritual life. Also, most will include family, security, and success. Success, unfortunately, is often measured in dollars instead of integrity.

"COMMITMENTS: These are the hardest as they must come from the heart and are life changing. A simple example is a goal to be healthy. In essence, that requires exercising more and eating less and better—a struggle every day for many people. Likewise, a commitment to live as Christ wants us to live is a major change for the majority of us. Commitments are hard.

"PLANS: Plans are the easy part. If you keep your commitments, the plans fall into place.

"For much of my time as a POW and in my years since release from Hanoi in 1973, this simple formula has served me well."

Rank and organization
Lieutenant Colonel (then Maj.), U.S. Air Force,
357th Tactical Fighter Squadron.
Place and date
Over North Vietnam, 19 April 1967.

CITATION

For conspicuous gallantry and intrepidity in action at the risk of his life above and beyond the call of duty. As pilot of an F-105 aircraft, Lt. Col. Thorsness was on a surface-to-air missile suppression mission over North Vietnam. Lt. Col. Thorsness and his wingman attacked and silenced a surface-to-air missile site with air-to-ground missiles, and then destroyed a second surface-to-air missile site with bombs. In the attack on the second missile site, Lt. Col. Thorsness' wingman was shot down by intensive antiaircraft fire, and the 2 crewmembers abandoned their aircraft. Lt. Col. Thorsness circled the descending parachutes to keep the crewmembers in sight and relay their position to the Search and Rescue Center.

During this maneuver, a MIG-17 was sighted in the area. Lt. Col. Thorsness immediately initiated an attack and destroyed the MIG. Because his aircraft was low on fuel, he was forced to depart the area in search of a tanker. Upon being advised that 2 helicopters were orbiting over the downed crew's position and that there were hostile MIGs in the area posing a serious threat to the helicopters, Lt. Col. Thorsness, despite his low fuel condition, decided to return alone through a hostile environment of surface-to-air missile and antiaircraft defenses to the downed crew's position.

As he approached the area, he spotted 4 MIG-17 aircraft and immediately initiated an attack on the MIGs, damaging 1 and driving the others away from the rescue scene. When it became apparent that an aircraft in the area was critically low on fuel and the crew would have to abandon the aircraft unless they could reach a tanker, Lt. Col. Thorsness, although critically short on fuel himself, helped to avert further possible loss of life and a friendly aircraft by recovering at a forward operating base, thus allowing the aircraft in emergency fuel condition to refuel safely.

Lt. Col. Thorsness' extraordinary heroism, self-sacrifice, and personal bravery involving conspicuous risk of life were in the highest traditions of the military service and have reflected great credit upon himself and the U.S. Air Force.

———•◦••◦•———

PEOPLE OR TRUCKS

I taxied with two F-105s fighters to the end of the runway at Takhli, Thailand, in January 1967. I had about 50 Wild Weasel missions over North Vietnam in my assigned mission to seek out and destroy surface-to-air missile (SAM) sites.

We had the standard wait at the end of the runway while the ground crews armed our guns, bombs, and air-to-ground missiles. The wait was especially long as several aircraft were landing. As we waited to take the runway, my backseater and I talked about the Thai peasants who were working at the end of the runway. It seemed the women were doing most of the work while the men were hunkering and smoking cigarettes. We couldn't hear the conversation, of course, but it was obvious that none were working too hard and were having a good time as they laughed, pointed, and exchanged lots of banter. Harry, my backseater, and I commented that it was nice they were enjoying life.

All North Vietnamese SAMs were normally kept within a hundred miles of Hanoi or so. Occasionally they would sneak one down by the DMZ to get a shot at a B-52 or refueling tanker. There were overnight reports from electronic intelligence aircraft that the North Vietnamese may have sneaked a SAM just north of the DMZ. Our early morning mission was to see if it was there and destroy it.

My wingman and I made the 40 minute flight to the southern part of North Vietnam. We crisscrossed several times the narrow span of North Vietnam between Laos and the Gulf of Tonkin without picking up any electric signals of the SAM's radar.

We stayed at least 10,000 feet above a low, solid cloud cover so if they quickly launched a SAM, we would have time to see and outmaneuver it. We saw no SAMs and heard no signals and were getting close to our low fuel depart time. Just then, faster than I'd seen, the solid but thin, low cloud layer quickly burned off from the early morning sun. I dropped down to about 5,000 feet for a better visual inspection of the suspected SAM site. What I saw instead were hundreds of North Vietnamese working to repair the previous day's bomb damage to Highway 1, the North Vietnamese main route for supplies from Hanoi to the South. The workers were out in the open; a perfect target for my CBU bombs. CBUs are mother bombs that, when dropped, have a shell that opens and about a thousand hand grenade sized bomblets spew out and explode when hitting the ground. CBUs are perfect weapons for thin-skinned things like missiles and people.

It was nearly time to head home, and we found a perfectly legitimate target—North Vietnamese helping get supplies to their troops in South Vietnam to fight and kill Americans. I looked over the area and about a mile north of the peasants were several trucks and busses—obviously transport for the workers.

I made a radio call, "Cadillac two, afterburner NOW; go bomb mode." I pulled my nose up and climbed for 18,000 feet to roll on a bomb run. In the few seconds it took to climb, my wingman called, "Cadillac lead, what's the target?"

We had two legitimate targets—people or trucks—and we had the right weapons for either. While reaching for 18,000 feet, the image of happy Thai workers we had watched just an hour ago flashed in my mind. Here were similar people, living under communism, forced to work in an open area filling bomb craters, and fearing they were about to be bombed. My mind said the best target was the peasants; my heart said it was the trucks. The Thai peasants image stayed in my mind. The entire thought process lasted the few seconds I had before deciding the target: people or trucks.

As vividly as if it were yesterday, I recall turning my head and looking at my left shoulder. There sat Jesus Christ. I asked, "People or trucks?" As quickly as I asked, He answered, "Trucks."

As we rolled over inverted and started pulling our nose earthward into a bomb run, I called, "Cadillac two, we hit the trucks!"

—*Leo Thorsness*

Part 2

Scriptures for Those Who Serve

WWII U.S. Army 10th Corps Shoulder Sleeve Insignia

The Tenth Corps saw action in the Pacific in WWII and again in the Korean War. In many armies, a corps is composed of two or more divisions. During WWI and WWII, multiple corps were combined into armies, and armies were formed into Army Groups. In most Western armies, corps are numbered using Roman numerals.

THE TEN COMMANDMENTS: Exodus 20:3-17
and their hand/finger signals

I. There is only 1 God. Have no other gods...
Thou shall have no other gods before me. v.3

II. Don't worship idols. *(Don't bow down.)*
Thou shall not bow down to them, nor serve them. v.5

III. Do not take the name of the Lord (Trinity) in vain. *(Each finger represents One of the Trinity, fingers touching lips.) Thou shall not take the name of thy God in vain.* v.7

IV. Remember the Sabbath *(Thumb is resting in the palm of the hand.) Remember the Sabbath day and keep it holy.* v.8

V. I pledge to honor my father and mother. *Honor thy father and thy mother.* v.12

VI. Thou shalt not kill *(Finger pointing to murder). Thou shall not murder.* v.13

VII. Love only your husband and wife. *(Thumbs and index fingers form a heart.) Thou shall not commit adultery.* v.14

VIII. Thou shall not steal. *(Fingers represent prison bars, fingers placed over eyes.) Thou shall not steal.* v.15

IX. Thou shall not lie. *(Hands over mouth.) Thou shall not bear false witness.* v.16

X. Thou shall not look at things and want them. *(Hands over eyes.) Thou shall not covet.* v.17

Civil War and Current Navy Good Conduct Medals

The Good Conduct Medal is one of our nation's oldest military awards. The Navy Good Conduct Medal was first issued in 1869, followed by the Marine medal in 1896, the Coast Guard in 1923, and the Army in 1941. The Air Force created its version of the Good Conduct Medal in 1963.

The word "fidelity" is the one common word embossed on each branch of the service Good Conduct medal. The definition of fidelity is loyalty and faithfulness. In the book, *VALOR*, COL Robert Howard, MOH, Vietnam and CAPT Thomas Hunder, MOH, Korea, offer the following wisdom about loyalty:

A soldier cannot be truly loyal to his superiors unless he is loyal to his subordinates and peers. —*Robert Howard*

A leader must be loyal to his juniors (his subordinates), as well as his seniors (his superiors). Loyalty down begets loyalty up. It is loyalty among comrades in the field that succeeds in battle and wins the war." —*Tom Hudner*

Exodus 17:8-13

Then Amalek came and fought with Israel in Rephidim. Moses said to Joshua, "Choose men for us, and go out and fight with Amalek.

Tomorrow I will stand on the top of the hill with God's rod in my hand." So Joshua did as Moses had told him, and fought with Amalek; and Moses, Aaron, and Hur went up to the top of the hill. It happened, when Moses held up his hand, that Israel prevailed; and when he let down his hand, Amalek prevailed. But Moses' hands were heavy; and they took a stone, and put it under him, and he sat on it. Aaron and Hur held up his hands, the one on the one side, and the other on the other side. His hands were steady until sunset. Joshua defeated Amalek and his people with the edge of the sword.

Moses was faithful to God by keeping his arms raised. As long as his arms were raised, Joshua and the Israelite army prevailed; but when Moses could no longer keep his arms up, Aaron and Hur came alongside Moses and helped him keep his arms raised to God. Moses was faithful to God but needed the help of Aaron and Hur. These two men are examples of loyalty and faithfulness to God, to Moses, and to Joshua in the defeat of Amalek.

For those who serve in uniform, loyalty and faithfulness to service and their units are of profound importance. Loyalty and faithfulness to family and friends are also of profound importance. And of course, above all else, we all owe loyalty and faithfulness to God.

US Army Sergeants Major Academy
and the US Army War College Shoulder Sleeve Insignia

The Sergeants Major Academy was established in 1972 at Fort Bliss, TX. The US Army War College was established in 1901 and is located in Carlisle, PA.

Retired Air Force General Lloyd Newton offered this advice for *A Gathering of Eagles:* "Always strive to learn something new. If we are not learning something new each day, we should consider it an incomplete day."

The importance of knowledge, wisdom, and understanding are addressed in countless books. In Proverbs 4:7 we read, "Getting wisdom is the most important thing you can do. Whatever else you get, get wisdom." We have a human obligation to share knowledge with those who follow after us. But it is even more important to share spiritual wisdom with our children. Sharing our spiritual knowledge has an eternal impact. We are directed to teach our children as it says in Deuteronomy 6:7.

Deuteronomy—the 5th book of the Bible, the 6th chapter, the 7th verse:

And thou teach them diligently to thy children, and thou shall talk of them when you sit down in your house, and when you walk by the way, and when you lie down and when you get up (Deut. 6:7).

Unauthorized Jacket Pocket Patches
Afghanistan and Iraq

The current Eagle, Globe, and Anchor insignia of the Marine Corps traces its roots to the design worn by Marines in 1776. In 1868, it was recommended that the globe showing the western hemisphere intersected by a fouled anchor and surmounted by a spread eagle be the emblem of the Marine Corps. The banner clasped in the eagle's beak bears the Latin motto, *Semper Fidelis,* which means, "Always Faithful."

It is sometimes said that the most important word in the motto is "always"—not sometimes, not most of the time, but always—always faithful, during the good times or difficult times.

In II Timothy 2:13 we read, "If we are faithless, He abideth faithful; for He cannot deny Himself" (ASV). At times in life we wander from the faith, but God is faithful, always waiting for us to return to the faith and to Him. In John 3:16 (b), we find the hope that God offers us with the statement, "That whosoever believeth on Him, should not perish but have eternal life."

Deuteronomy 7:9

Know therefore that the Lord thy God, he is God, the faithful God, which keepeth covenant and mercy with them that love him and keep his commandments to a thousand generations.

MSG Andy Coy, COL Jim Coy, and CSM Eldon Coy

BE STRONG AND OF GOOD COURAGE

My two brothers and I served for a total of 93 years in the Army. They were great mentors. One was decorated for valor in Vietnam and the other for heroism.

In *VALOR*, Colonel Carl Sitter, USMC, (Ret) addressed courage with the statement, "There are two types of courage: physical and moral courage. The former is by far the more common of the two. Moral courage sustains us in a mental crisis because it gives a person the courage of their convictions."

In *A Gathering of Eagles*, Colonel Travis Hoover, the second pilot to fly off the aircraft carrier, Hornet, in the Doolittle Raid, offered these thoughts about courage. "My mother taught me about bravery and courage. She frequently admonished me to always have the courage to do the right thing regardless of the cost. Her advice left me with the commitment to always have the courage to do the right thing."

Captain Eugene McDaniel, USN, (Ret) was a POW in Vietnam. He was severely beaten by his captors. He offered this thought about courage in the video, *Prisoners of Hope*: "Courage is not the absence of fear but the presence of faith."

Navy Captain Thomas Kelly, (Ret) received the Medal of Honor in Vietnam. In his advice for life in *VALOR*, he said, "Knowing the right thing to do is usually easy. Doing the right thing is often very tough."

May God give us the courage to make and keep our commitment to Him!

Joshua 1:19

Have not I commanded thee? Be strong and of a good courage; be not afraid, neither be thou dismayed; for the Lord thy God is with thee wherever you go.

Army Infantry School Shoulder Sleeve Insignia

FOLLOW ME

The home of the U.S. Army Infantry School is located at Fort Benning, GA. The school teaches more than thirty different initial entry courses for every branch of the military. The school also has students from many allied nations of the world. The motto of the school is: FOLLOW ME.

Joshua followed Moses as the leader of the Hebrew nation, and he led the people into the Promised Land. His statement, "We will serve the Lord" is one of the greatest "Follow Me" statements of the Christian faith.

Jesus said to His future disciples, "Follow me, and I will make you fishers of men." (Matthew 4:19)

Joshua 24:15

And if it seem evil to you to serve the Lord, choose you this day who you will serve; whether the gods which your fathers served that were on the other side of the flood, or the gods of the Amorites, in whose land you dwell: But as for me and my house, we will serve the Lord.

II, VII, XIV Corps Shoulder Sleeve Insignia

The Second Corps saw action in Europe in WWI and WWII. The Seventh Corps saw action in Europe in WWI, WWII, and again in the Persian Gulf War. The Fourteenth Corps saw action in the Pacific in WWII. Typically a Corps is composed of 20,000 to 45,000 soldiers. Two to five divisions usually constitute a Corps, which is most often commanded by a Lieutenant General.

LTG Richard Graves had a long and distinguished career in the U.S. Army. He was a graduate of West Point, class of 1961, a Rhodes Scholar, and earned additional degrees from Oxford. General Graves served in the Dominican Republic and in Vietnam. He was the 54th Superintendent of West Point. Following his retirement from the Army in 1996, he became the 11th Chancellor of the Texas A&M University system. In *A Gathering of Eagles,* he offered this advice:

> Leaders must have integrity because we are in positions of trust. It is important that we have a sincere concern for our fellow men and women because, frankly, we are not here for ourselves, as individuals or as institutions. We are here for a greater cause—to glorify God and serve others.

In our effort to glorify God, we must be willing to humble ourselves and pray. The essence of Romans 1:21-28 is: Because they knew God but glorified him not as God, neither were they thankful, and their hearts and minds were darkened. We must be willing to glorify God and thank Him. As individuals and as a nation, we must humble ourselves and pray...only then will He heal our land.

2 Chronicles 7:14

If my people who are called by my name, shall humble themselves and pray, and seek my face, and turn from their wicked ways; then will I hear from heaven, and will forgive their sin, and will heal their land.

35th Transportation Bn., 3rd Infantry Division Pocket Patch, 11th Armored Cavalry Regiment, and Army Acquisition Corps Shoulder Sleeve Insignia

CHARIOTS, HORSES, AND THE LORD

"I am the alpha and omega" (Rev. 1:8). Alpha and omega are the first and last letters of the classical Greek alphabet. Many Bible commentaries apply this title to both God and to Christ.

Many years ago, I attended a revival at a local church where a well-known evangelist was speaking. During the service, he turned and looked directly at me and said, "I have a word from God for you. The word is from Proverbs 3:5-6. 'Trust in the Lord with all your heart; and lean not unto your own understanding. In all your ways acknowledge him, and He will direct thy paths.'"

I had never experienced anything like that before. I was told later that I should accept it as a prophetic word. Since that time I have claimed that word from God for my life. Trusting in God and having faith and hope in God offers great peace.

Over the years, I have met many individuals who consider these verses from Proverbs as important verses by which to live. Desmond Doss and Mitchell Paige—whose stories are included in this book—both received the Medal of Honor in WWII. Trusting in God was of profound importance for each of them. Totally trusting in God every day, in the good times, the difficult times, and yes, even in the bad times, provides great comfort and peace.

I would like to offer the same word from God to you. "Trust in the Lord with all your heart...He will direct your paths."

Psalm 20:7

Some trust in chariots, and some trust in horses; But we will trust in the name of the Lord God (Psalm 20:7).

WWII Pathfinder Cloth Forearm Sleeve Insignia and Current Pathfinder Badge

The origin of the original Pathfinder units occurred during WWII. Small groups of airborne-qualified soldiers were formed into pathfinder units. The mission of these units was to parachute into enemy territory ahead of the main force to mark drop zones and landing zones. The possibility of capture behind enemy lines was considered great in these units. Because of the sensitive and often secret mission of the units, it was determined that wearing the pathfinder insignia would only be allowed with the dress uniform. The cloth pathfinder insignia was worn on the left sleeve of the dress uniform at or below the level of the elbow.

In V*ALOR*, Brian Thacker offered this statement: "I am often asked, 'What did you think about, and what gave you the most comfort during the eight days that you were alone and surrounded by the enemy, knowing they were continually searching to find you?' My answer might sound a little odd because I am not really a 'church person,' but the three things that gave me the most comfort were the Lord's Prayer, the 23rd Psalm, and the first few lines from the poem *Invictus.*'"

PSALM 23

The Lord is my shepherd; I shall not want. He maketh me to lie down in green pastures: he leadeth me beside the still waters. He restoreth my soul: he leadeth me in the paths of righteousness for his name's sake. Yea, though I walk through the valley of the shadow of death, I will fear no evil: for thou art with me; thy rod and thy staff they comfort me. Thou preparest a table before me in the presence of mine enemies: thou anointest my head with oil; my cup runneth over. Surely goodness and mercy shall follow me all the days of my life: and I will dwell in the house of the Lord for ever.

WWI and WWII 91st Division Shoulder Sleeve Insignia

The 91st Infantry Division, at times called the "Pine Tree Division" or the "Wild West Division," fought in WWI and WWII and is currently an Army Reserve Training Division.

THE SOLDIER'S PRAYER—Psalm 91:1-16

He that dwells in the secret place of the Most High shall abide under the shadow of the Almighty. I will say of the Lord, He is my refuge and my fortress; My God, in whom I trust. For he will deliver thee from the snare of the fowler, and from the deadly pestilence. He will cover thee with his feathers, and under his wings shall thou take refuge: His truth is a shield and buckler. Thou shall not be afraid for the terror by night, nor the arrow that flies by day; For the pestilence that walks in darkness, nor for the destruction that lays waste at noonday. A thousand shall fall at thy side, and ten thousand at thy right hand; but it shall not come nigh thee. Only with your eyes shall you see the reward of the wicked. For thou O Lord, art my refuge! Thou has made the Most High your habitation; There shall no evil befall thee, neither shall any plague come near thy dwelling. For he will give his angels charge over thee, to keep thee in all thy ways. They shall bear thee up in their hands, lest you dash your foot against a stone. Thou shall tread upon the lion and the cobra: the young lion and the serpent shall you trample under foot. Because he hath set his love upon me, therefore will I deliver him: I will set him on high, because he hath known my name. He shall call upon me, and I will answer him; I will be with him in trouble: I will deliver him, and honor him. With long life will I satisfy him, and show him my salvation.

160th Army Special Operations Aviation Regiment (Airborne)
The Night Stalkers and
VF – 101 Navy Fighter Squadron Flight Suit Patches

The 160th is a Special Operations aviation unit of the United States Army. The unit is known as the "Night Stalkers." It is composed of some of the best trained and equipped aviators and soldiers in the Army. The motto of the unit is, "Night Stalkers Don't Quit."

The unit has deployed all over the world and has seen combat in Grenada, Panama, Southwest Asia and numerous other Armed Forces Expeditionary missions.

The VF – 101 Naval Fighter Squadron was named the "Grim Reapers" and was originally activated in 1942 and deployed to the South Pacific during WWII. VF – 101 again saw action in the Korean War.

Psalm 91:5-7

Thou shall not be afraid for the terror by night; nor for the arrow that flies by day; Nor for the pestilence that walks in darkness; nor for the destruction that lays waste at noonday. A thousand shall fall at thy side, and ten thousand at thy right hand; but it shall not come near thee (Psalms 91:5-7).

XXIII Corps and 30th Artillery Brigade Shoulder Sleeve Insignia

The 23rd Corps served in Europe in WWII. The colors of blue and white indicate Corps colors. The division of the oval into two along with the three arrows indicated the unit's numerical designation of twenty-three.

The 30th Artillery Brigade shoulder sleeve insignia was approved in 1966. It was re-designated as the 30th Air Defense Artillery Brigade in 1972. The colors of gold/yellow represent Air

Defense Artillery. The three arrows and the circle that simulates a target represent the numerical designation.

Psalm 127:3-5

Children are a heritage of the Lord...As arrows in the hand of a mighty man; so are children of thy youth. They shall meet the enemies at the gate.

Part of my daily prayers includes praying for my family and for future generations. In Proverbs 17:6, we read, "A children's children are the crown of old men." Children are a blessing from God, but our grandchildren are an extra-special blessing!

I assume everyone who believes in prayer and has children spends some time praying for them. Over the years I have decided to pray for at least five future generations. As I pray a blessing on them, I pray for my children and grandchildren. I then pray for their children, and their children, and their children, and their children, and their children, and all who follow after them. My prayer is that they will know and serve the Lord. I pray for them human success; but more importantly, I pray for spiritual significance.

My biblical reference for this habit is from II Kings 13:14-19. The story is the about the king of Israel and the prophet Elisha. In verse 18, Elisha tells the king of Israel to "smite his arrows on the ground." The king then struck the ground with his arrows three times. In verse 19, we read that Elisha was extremely upset with the king, saying, "You should have struck the arrows on the ground five or six times; had you done this you would have defeated your enemies forever. Now you will only defeat your enemy three times."

It is essential that we pass along our Christian faith to our children. Our ability and success in doing this will have an eternal impact on them and those who follow after them.

Our Christian faith will allow our children, their children, and those who follow after them, to fight and obtain victory in the spiritual battles. In Joel 1:3 we read, "Tell your children of it, and let your children tell their children, and their children another generation." In *Prisoners of Hope*, retired Navy Captain Eugene "Red" McDaniel who was a POW in Vietnam for over six years, offered this wisdom: "Without battle, no man can come to victory; the greater the battle, the greater the victory."

Passing our faith in God to our children is addressed in the last verse of the Old Testament that is the transition verse into the New Testament. In Malachi 4:5, we find this command and warning; "He shall turn the heart of the fathers to their children, and the heart of the children to their fathers, lest I come and smite the earth with a curse."

WWII RANGER Shoulder Sleeve Insignia and 5th Ranger Scroll Insignia

OMAHA BEACH, JUNE 6TH, 1944
"RANGERS, LEAD THE WAY"

Brigadier General Norman Cota was the Assistant Division Commander of the 29th Infantry Division. He landed with the second wave on Omaha beach during the D-Day invasion. A famous quote attributed to him on D-Day is when he asked a soldier, "What outfit is this?" Someone yelled back, "5th Rangers!" Cota replied, "Well...then, Rangers, lead the way." The brief exchange led to the Ranger motto: "Rangers lead the way."

Having God go before you and as your rear guard offers great comfort to all who have faith and hope in the Lord.

Isaiah 52:12

For the LORD will go before you; and the God of Israel will be your rear guard.

Colonel Insignia—Civil War and present

In 1832, gold eagles were authorized for Infantry Colonels in the American Army. Silver eagles were worn by Colonels in all other branches of the Army. In 1851, the Army changed the regulation and all Colonels were authorized and required to wear silver eagles.

WITH WINGS AS EAGLES—Isaiah 40:31

For they that WAIT upon the Lord shall renew their strength. They shall mount up with wings as eagles; they shall run, and not be weary, and they shall walk, and not faint (KJV).

But those who HOPE in the Lord will renew their strength. They will soar on wings like eagles; they will run and not grow weary, they will walk and not be faint (NIV).

But those who TRUST in the Lord will find new strength. They will soar high on wings like eagles. They will run and not grow weary. They will walk and not faint (NLT).

Those who WAIT, HOPE, and TRUST in the Lord will renew their strength.

Blessed is the man who TRUSTS in the Lord, and whose HOPE is in the Lord (Jer. 17:7-8).

123rd Signal Battalion Pocket Patch (1950s)

AS EASY AS ONE, TWO, THREE

The 123rd Signal Battalion has its origin as the 4th and then the 5th Signal Battalion of the Signal Corps and initially served in WWI in support of the 3rd Infantry Division in France. The unit was activated again and served in WWII in Africa and then in Europe as the 3rd Signal Company. The 3rd also served in Korea during the Korean War. After the Korean War, the unit was reorganized and re-designated as the 123rd Signal Battalion, serving in Bosnia-Herzegovina in 2000. In 2003, elements of the 123rd deployed in support of the 3rd Infantry Division as part of Operation Iraqi Freedom.

In *A Gathering of Eagles,* former Senator James Talent offered this statement; "Is there a God? Does He have a purpose for my life? How can I come to know Him and His plan for me? I found the answer to those questions in the death and resurrection of Jesus Christ."

Matthew 1:23

Behold, a virgin shall be with child, and shall bring forth a son, and they shall call his name Emmanuel, which interpreted is, God with us.

God loves us and He has a plan and a purpose for our lives. He sent us a sign...a signal through His Son, Jesus Christ. What an amazing blessing—God is with us!

Law Enforcement Pocket Patch

MY FATHER MY HERO

Bill Owens, former Governor of Colorado, offered the following advice for life in the book, *A Gathering of Eagles.*

The most important lessons I learned on moving from success to significance I learned from my father. My father spent his entire life blessing me with his knowledge and experience.

As a man he taught me to be good, proud, honest, and above all, remain true to oneself and one's beliefs. He also taught me the importance of hard work, congeniality, and perseverance. As a husband, he taught me to respect women, to treat them as equals. As a father, he taught me the enormous impact unconditional love and support can have on a child's life.

Roger Donlon was the first recipient of the Medal of Honor in Vietnam. He offered the following Irish proverb for the book, *VALOR*: "What we are is God's gift to us; what we become is our gift to God."

The blessing of our spiritual Father and our earthly father makes it possible for us to move from success to significance.

Matthew 6:9-13—The Lord's Prayer

Our Father which art in heaven, Hallowed be thy name. Thy kingdom come. Thy will be done in earth, as it is in heaven. Give us this day our daily bread. And forgive us our debts, as we forgive our debtors. And lead us not into temptation, but deliver us from evil: For thine is the kingdom, and the power, and the glory, forever. Amen.

WWII KISKA Task Force Shoulder Sleeve Insignia

The Training and Doctrine Command (TRADOC) definition of fratricide is the employment of friendly weapons and munitions with the intent to kill the enemy or destroy his equipment or facilities, which results in unforeseen and unintentional death or injury to friendly personnel.

The KISKA Task Force was composed of 35,000 United States and Canadian troops. The combined unit made an assault on Kiska, in the Aleutian Islands, on August 1943. The assault was complicated by dense fog. The fighting continued throughout the day and into the night. By the end of the fight a day later, 28 men were dead and 50 were wounded. The problem—there were no Japanese on the island. One hundred percent of the casualties were fratricide. Fratricide is one of the ever-present tragedies of war. Wounding and killing of fellow soldiers is one of the horrible realities of war.

It seems odd, but a similar comparison can be made in the family of faith. The reality is that different churches have different approaches to our Christian faith. There are many different denominations, doctrines, and tenets, yet we all believe in the One God, His Son, and the Holy Spirit. Even with our similarities and common faith, we still cause spiritual injuries and wounds to others of faith. We do this with our words and actions. It is of profound importance that we do not commit spiritual fratricide. It is important that we do not injure and wound other true believers. I guess it is stated well in the Gospel of Thumper..."If you can't say something nice, don't say nothing at all."

Matthew 7:12

Therefore all things whatsoever you would that men should do to you, do even so to them: for this is the law and the prophets (see also Luke 6:31).

Five Star General Insignia

In December 1944, the Five-Star officer rank was created. Only nine men have achieved this rank. Interestingly, George Washington holds the honor of having the highest rank in U.S. military history with the title, General of the Armies of the United States. This title and honor was awarded after his death.

In *A Gathering of Eagles,* former Governor Mike Huckabee of Arkansas offers this evaluation of leadership:

> The ultimate evaluation of effective leadership is not determined by how many people serve us, but rather, how many people we serve.

When I think of the meaning of leadership, I am reminded of two basic tenets. The first: To lead, you must first know how to follow. The second: Never ask someone to do something that you are not willing to do.

The essence of true leadership is central to the statement by Jesus in Matthew 20:28.

Matthew 20:28

I did not come to be served but to serve.

Original and Current Special Operations
Medical Association Challenge Coins

Many military organizations use challenge coins. Service members carry their coin with pride. There are many stories about challenge coins, what they mean, how they are used, and their origin.

The origin of the Challenge Coin is often attributed to an Army Air Service unit in WWI. As the story goes, one aviator had coins minted for every aviator in his unit with the unit insignia.

During WWI, one of the pilots from that unit was shot down and captured. His identification papers and dog tag were confiscated upon capture. That night, the pilot escaped from his captors and was picked up by the French. They were concerned that he was a German saboteur and considered executing him.

Since he was unable to give them any military identification, he showed them the coin. They recognized the U.S. Army Air Service insignia on the coin and returned him to his unit.

TWO COINS WITH A CHALLENGE

1864 Two-Cent Piece

The two-cent coin was minted and circulated from 1864–1873. During the American Civil War, there was real concern about the future of the nation. Concerned how the nation might be remembered, Abraham Lincoln requested the chief engraver of the United States Mint to create a coin with the motto, "In God We Trust." The 1864 two-cent piece was the very first U.S. coin to bear that motto.

Tiberius Tribute Penny Roman Coin

In Matthew 22:17-22, we read about Jesus' response to the crowd when he was asked, "Is it right to give tax to Caesar, or not?" His response, "Show me a coin." When someone offered him a coin, he asked, "Whose image is on the coin?" The crowd responded, "Caesar's." Then he replied, "Give to Caesar the things which are Caesar's, and to God the things which are God's."

The military challenge coin offers us the opportunity to recognize service and pride with a specific unit or organization. The motto on the two-cent piece and the statement by Jesus about the Roman coin challenge us to remember the importance of acknowledging and serving God.

We frequently say, "God bless America." Some people change the adage to: "America, bless God." May you always remember your priorities for service.

Matthew 22:21

Render therefore unto Caesar the things which are Caesar's; and unto God the things that are God's.

WWI and WWII 1st Infantry Division Shoulder Sleeve Insignia

The 1st Infantry Division is the oldest division in the United States Army. It is officially nicknamed "The Big Red One." Interestingly, the division was the first unit to deploy to Europe in WWI and was named the First Expeditionary Division, later renamed the 1st Division. In WWII, the unit first saw action in North Africa. The Division was the first to land on the beaches during the invasion of Sicily and also the first to land in France on D-Day at Omaha Beach. The 1st Division was also the first division to deploy to Vietnam in 1965.

Joe Foss was the leading fighter ace of the United States Marine Corps during WWII. He received the Medal of Honor, was a governor of South Dakota, the president of numerous organizations, TV personality, and author. In *VALOR*, Foss made this statement; "I frequently speak to different groups and am often asked the question, 'Of all the honors and awards that you have received, what do you consider the most important, number one?' I look them in the eye and say, 'The day that I invited Jesus Christ into my life as my Lord and Savior is number one."

In life we are often asked, what is most important? What is number one in your life? I appreciate the advice for life offered by Admiral Jerry Denton. "I strive for the ultimate significant success—heaven—by loving and serving God, family, and country."

In Luke 12:34 we read, "For where your treasure is, there will your heart be also." Saint Augustine offered these thoughts on the scripture writing: "Where your pleasure is, there is your treasure; where your treasure is, there is your heart; where your heart is, there is your happiness."

Where is your pleasure, your treasure, your heart, your happiness? What is the greatest, the number one priority, or the most important thing in your life?

Deuteronomy 6:5; Matthew 22:37-39; Mark 12:31

And thou shalt love the Lord thy God with all thine heart, and with all thy soul, and with all thy might (Deut. 6:5).

When Jesus was asked, "What is the greatest commandment?" He replied, "Thou shall love the Lord thy God with all thy heart, and with all thy soul, and with all thy mind. This is the first and greatest commandment. And the second is like unto it, Thou shall love thy neighbor as thyself (Matt. 22:37-39; see also Luke 10:27).

And the second is like, namely this, Thou shalt love thy neighbour as thyself. There is none other commandment greater than these (Mark 12:31).

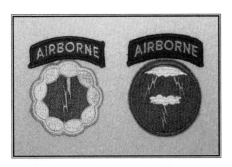

9th and 21st WWII Airborne Division Shoulder Sleeve Insignia
Phantom Divisions – Operation Fortitude

The 9th and 21st Airborne Divisions are two phantom units created on paper as part of Operation Fortitude. "Ghost" Army and "Phantom" Divisions were created during WWII to confuse the German military about the true numbers, units, and location of the D-Day invasion. The deception included fake military installations and equipment in southern England, fake radio message traffic, and false information fed to German intelligence to suggest the invasion would happen at Pas-de-Calis in France. Shoulder sleeve insignia were approved for two corps and nineteen phantom divisions to confuse the enemy. General George Patton was named as the Commanding General in the deception.

Lightning bolts are commonly used in the insignia of numerous military units. Lightning bolts depict speed and surprise.

Matthew 24:27
For as lightning comes out of the east, and shines to the west; so shall be the coming of the Son of man.

Romans 14:11
Every Christian looks forward to the return of Christ with the belief that "Every knee will bow and every tongue will confess that Jesus Christ is Lord."

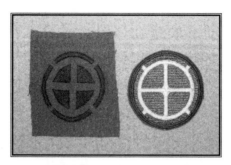

35th Division, "The Santa Fe"
WWI and WWII Shoulder Sleeve Insignia

My two brothers both began their military service in the Missouri Army National Guard with the 35th Infantry Division. I also spent two years in the 35th Infantry Division (Mechanized) as the DISCOM Surgeon. I have a real sense of pride that we all served with this unit. At one point in time, each of us wore the 35th Infantry Division wagon wheel shoulder sleeve insignia.

The 35th served honorably in the Mexican Revolution, WWI, WWII, and in Kosovo. The shoulder sleeve insignia is a white wagon wheel with four spokes on a blue disc. The wagon wheel configuration reflects service and training along the Santa Fe Trail during WWI.

In the same way that the spokes of a wagon wheel maintain stability and strength for the journey, so too do the four spokes of the wheel of evangelism hold true for our journey as followers of Christ. These include: Being in the Word of God, being in prayer, being in fellowship with others of faith, and witnessing every day.

The following is advice for life from Billy Graham in *A Gathering of Eagles.*

Be faithful in whatever place God puts you. Pace your life according to the will and plan of God for you. Do not become impatient or try to go ahead of God. His track record is without failure, while our efforts can only end in frustration. Be determined to live your life with Jesus Christ at the center, enjoying daily times of prayer and Bible study. Be sure to share your faith regularly, meet with others of faith, and trust God to lead you step by step in a life that is totally yielded to Him."

Matthew 28:16

Then the eleven disciples went away into Galilee, into a mountain where Jesus had appointed them.

WWII Army Air Force Flight Surgeon Badge and Current Army Flight Surgeon Badge

AVIATION THEOLOGY
Boeing 737 and 747 aircraft

The flight surgeon is a military physician or physician's assistant whose primary duty is the medical evaluation, certification, and treatment of military aviation personnel. The term "flight surgeon" originated in early 1918 when the United States Air Medical Service of the U.S. Army was given the task of evaluation of and caring for U.S. military aviators.

And, behold a woman in the city, which was a sinner, when she knew that Jesus sat to eat in the Pharisee's house, brought an alabaster box of ointment, and stood at his feet behind him weeping, and began to wash his feet with tears, and wiped them with the hairs of her head, and kiss his feet, and anointed them with ointment. Now when the Pharisee saw this, he spoke to himself, saying, If this man is really a prophet he would have known who and what kind of woman this is that touched him: for she is a sinner. And Jesus answering said unto him, Simon, I have something to say to you. And he said, Master, tell me.

There was a certain creditor which had two debtors: the one owed five hundred shillings and the other fifty. And when they had nothing to pay, he forgave them both the debt. Tell me, which one of them will love the master the most? Simon answered and said, I suppose that he who he forgive the most. And he responded, You are correct.

And he turned to the woman, and said to Simon. See this woman? I entered your home, and you gave me no water to wash my feet: but she has washed my feet with her tears, and them wiped them with the hair of her head. You gave me no kiss: but this woman from the time I came in has not ceased to kiss my feet. My head you did not anoint with oil: but she has anointed my feet with ointment. Wherefore I say to you, her sins, which are many are forgiven; for she loved much: but to whom little is forgiven, the same loves little (Luke 7:37-47).

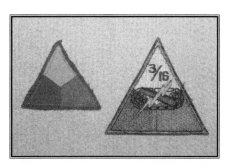

WWI Armor Shoulder Sleeve Insignia and (3rd Squadron of the 16th Armored Cavalry) 3/16 Armored Cavalry –
Unauthorized Pocket Patch

The triangular shape and color arrangement of the 3/16 Armor patch is historically credited as being approved by General George Patton when he was a young tank corps officer in WWI. The color yellow traditionally represents Cavalry, blue is for Infantry, and red for Artillery. Armored units are often designated with a number at the top of the patch.

(Interestingly, most online Bible resources indicate that John 3:16 is the most searched-for verse on their sites.)

John 3:16

For God so loved the world that He gave His only begotten Son, that whosoever believeth in him should not perish, but have everlasting life.

WWI and WWII 36th Division Shoulder Sleeve Insignia

The 36th Infantry Division, also known as the "Texas Division," is part of the Texas Army National Guard. The 36th served in Europe in WWII and in the Global War on Terror in Afghanistan and Iraq.

The capital letter "T" on the 36th Division shoulder sleeve insignia reminds me of the statement about truth with a capital letter T. In the evangelical Christian community, the word truth with a capital letter "T" refers to God's Truth. There is man's truth and God's Truth, but God's Truth is always truth.

Charles Coolidge served with the 36th Infantry Division during WWII. Mr. Coolidge received the Medal of Honor for action in France in 1944. In *VALOR*, he stated,

> Hill 623 in southern France will remain steadfast in my memory. The action that occurred there resulted in my being awarded the Medal of Honor, our country's highest military decoration. But I must be quick to state that the act that took place on a hill called Calvary far exceeds any victory that man can conceive. It was there that the Lord laid down his life for all who would believe and accept His gift of grace. Those who have a Christian faith believe that Jesus Christ laid down his life so we might be saved. We accept this as fact, as truth with a capital T.

In John 8:32, we read, "You will know the truth and the truth will set you free."

John 14:6

I am the way, the truth, and the Life: no man comes to the Father, but by me.

Navy/Marine, Air Force, and Army
Medal of Honor

NO GREATER LOVE

The Medal of Honor is the very highest military decoration awarded by the United States. It is awarded for valor during combat to individuals who demonstrate "conspicuous gallantry and intrepidity at the risk of his or her life above and beyond the call of duty while engaged in an action against an enemy of the United States."

I was blessed to interview 117 individuals who received the Medal of Honor for the book, *VALOR – A Gathering of Eagles.* Meeting these men was a great honor. After spending time with them, I was amazed at their bravery. I was also impressed by their humility. In *VALOR*, six of the men I interviewed told me how they covered a grenade with their body to save the lives of the men around them. As they spoke about their act of heroism, many referred to the Scripture verse in John 15:13. "Greater love hath no man than this, that a man lay down his life for his friends."

Every one of these men admit that they were willing to die so others might live. Desmond Doss saved the lives of 75 men on the Maeda escarpment during the Battle of Okinawa. He stated, "I prayed to God, over and over again. 'Lord, I am willing to die if you will allow me to save just one more man.'"

We see the same type of courage and willingness to die for another in the example of Jesus Christ. Jesus was willing to die on the cross for us. He was willing to sacrifice His life so men could have the opportunity of an eternity with Him. It is often said, Jesus died for all, but He would have been willing to die on the cross to save only one person. He died for you. He died for me. He died for everyone.

John 15:13

Greater love hath no man than this, that a man
lay down his life for his friends.

Purple Heart and Prisoner of War Medals

The Purple Heart medal is awarded to military personnel who are wounded or killed in any action against an enemy of the United States. The original concept for the award is credited to General George Washington in 1782. The medal, as it appears today, was created in 1931.

The Prisoner of War Medal was authorized by Congress in

1985. The medal can be awarded to any service member who was a Prisoner of War after April 5, 1917.

Less than one percent of Americans will ever serve in the military. An even smaller percentage will serve in combat. Very few Americans will ever be wounded in service to our nation and even fewer will become a prisoner of war.

In the spiritual battles of life, everyone is wounded. We are wounded by sin. "All have sinned and come short of the glory of God" (Romans 3:23). Some of us will not only be wounded but will be taken captive by the devil and the powers of darkness. In II Timothy 2:26, we read about the "snare of the devil" and being "taken captive by him." Spiritually, we are all potential recipients of the spiritual Purple Heart medal and spiritual Prisoner of War medal.

The way to overcome the wounds and captivity of the spiritual battle with the devil and the powers of darkness is found in Romans 10:9.

Romans 10:9

Confess with our mouth the Lord Jesus, and believe in our heart that God raised him from the dead, and we shall be saved.

*WWII Parachute Badge (with combat stars) 4 Combat Jumps
and Variation Non-Regulation WWII Chaplain's Parachute Badge*

The Army Parachute Test Platoon was formed on June 26, 1940. Over time, the cadre at the Airborne Training center offered this statement when they were asked, "If your main parachute doesn't open, how long do you have to deploy your reserve parachute?" Their response: "You have the rest of your life."

Those who serve with Airborne units take great pride in their heritage. One officer who spent his entire career as a paratrooper was asked at his retirement, "General, I guess you must like to jump out of planes?" He replied, "No, but I like to hang around with the people who do."

George Wood served as a Chaplain with the 505th Parachute Infantry Regiment during World War II and made four combat jumps. After the war, George served for many years as the 82nd Airborne Division Association Chaplain. In *A Gathering of Eagles*, Chaplain Wood referred to the significance of Ephesians 6:11-18, and the whole armor of God and its importance to the spiritual battle we are involved in every day.

Ephesians 6:11-18

Put on the whole armor of God, that ye may be able to stand against the wiles of the devil. For we wrestle not against flesh and blood, but against principalities, against powers, against the rulers of the darkness of this world, against spiritual wickedness in high places. Wherefore take unto you the whole armor of God, that ye may be able to withstand in the evil day, and having done all, to stand. Stand therefore, having your loins gird about with truth, and having on the breastplate of righteousness; And your feet shod with the preparation of the gospel of peace; above all, taking the shield of faith, wherewith ye shall be able to quench all the fiery darts of the wicked. And take the helmet of salvation, and the sword of the Spirit, which is the word of God; praying always with all prayer and supplication in the Spirit, and watching thereunto with all perseverance and supplication for all the saints.

79th Inf. Division, 32nd Artillery Brigade Shoulder Sleeve Insignia

The 79th Infantry Division was first activated in 1917. The unit saw action in the Meuse Argonne area where it was given the name of the "Cross of Lorraine" because of its defense of France. The 79th again saw action in France landing on Utah Beach in Normandy in 1944.

The 32nd Army Air & Missile Defense Command had its beginning during World War I as an Artillery Brigade and participated in action at the battles of St. Mihiel and the Meuse Argonne. In WWII, the unit was re-designated as the 32nd Anti-Aircraft Artillery battery and served in the South Pacific.

The shoulder insignia for these two units are in the classic shape of a shield. The 79th is blue for Infantry and has a two-barred patriarchal cross. The 32nd is red for Artillery and has two rows of arrows. The two insignia make a great display for Ephesians 6:16.

Although translations vary slightly in the way they phrase this verse, many including the King James Version, the Bible in Basic English, the World English Bible, and Young's Literal translation begins the verse with, "Above all, take the shield of faith." This makes it apparent that faith is of profound importance. It is like saying, "Most importantly, take the shield of faith."

Eph. 6:16; Heb. 11:1; Heb. 11:6; II Cor. 5:7

Above all, take the shield of FAITH, wherewith to quench the fiery darts of the wicked (Eph. 6:16).

FAITH is the substance of things hoped for, the evidence of things not seen (Heb. 11:1).

Without FAITH it is impossible to please God (Heb. 11:6).

We walk by FAITH, not by sight (II Cor. 5:7).

WWI and WWII 77th Infantry Division Shoulder Sleeve Insignia

FREEDOM IS NOT FREE

The motto of the American Ex-Prisoner of War Association is: "Freedom is not free." In *Prisoners of Hope*, the following statements are offered by three Ex-Prisoners of War.

"Honor your flag. It spells freedom – yours and mine – and that freedom comes at a terrible price." —*Clarence Larsen, WWII, Survivor of the Bataan Death March.*

"Dying for freedom is not the worst thing that could happen. No, dying for freedom and being forgotten is." —*Cordino Longiotti, WWII, Europe.*

"We must live up to America's sacred obligation to those who fought with honor and did not return home from foreign battlefields. They deserve to never be forgotten." —*Willis Meier, WWII, Europe.*

Figuratively speaking, the flag of freedom does not fly in the wind. It is blown by the final breath of over 2 million American men and women who sacrificed their lives for the cause of freedom.

The price of freedom comes at a great cost. It is paid for with blood, sweat, tears, suffering, sorrow, and death. The cost of human and spiritual freedom is the same. Those who came before us paid a great price for our human freedom.

The cost of spiritual freedom also comes at a great cost. Jesus Christ was willing to suffer and die for our spiritual freedom. In the New Testament books of Galatians and I Peter, we read about spiritual freedom and its cost.

Galatians 5:1, 5:13; and I Peter 2:16

Christ set us free to live a free life. So take your stand! Never let anyone put a harness of slavery on you (Galatians 5:1).

It is absolutely clear that God has called you to a free life. Just make sure that you don't use this freedom as an excuse to do whatever you want to do and destroy your freedom (Galatians 5:13).

Exercise your freedom by serving God, not by breaking the rules (I Peter 2:16).

The reality of these Scriptures is that Christ died for our freedom. He did not die for our freedom to do what is wrong but to do what is right. Some might say, "I have the right, the freedom, to burn the flag." But most of us also realize that with freedom we also have a responsibility, an obligation, to do what is right, not what is wrong.

WWI and WWII Quartermaster Collar/Lapel Branch Insignia

During WWII, William Mauldin served as a cartoonist with the magazine *Stars and Stripes*, sometimes referred to as the "American Soldiers Newspaper," during WWII. Mauldin is famous for his cartoon characters, "Willie and Joe." Mauldin once said of the Quartermaster, "They are hewers of wood and haulers of water, a counter of buttons and sorter of socks." The insignia includes an eagle, a wagon wheel with 13 stars, a sword, and a key.

GOD SHALL SUPPLY ALL YOUR NEEDS

As I worked on the book, *Prisoners of Hope,* I heard this theme over and over that faith, family, and friends are key elements for survival as a POW. I was also impressed with this statement by some of the Ex-POWs: "When God is all you have, that is when you realize God is all you need." During good times, difficult times, and horrible times—faith, family, and friends help us endure.

When all is said and done, however, our most important need, our greatest need, is the need for God. Jeremiah Denton was a POW in Vietnam for seven years and seven months. He endured torture, starvation, and many other forms of inhumane treatment from his captors. He speaks about the importance of faith, family, and friends to his survival. He also offered this statement for two of the *Eagles* series books, "If we continue to forget God's ultimate significance, then America will not survive." "It is God who shall supply all our need according to his riches in glory by Jesus Christ" (Philippians 4:19).

William "Sonny" Mottern was a POW in Germany in WWII. He served as the National Commander of the American Ex-POW Association from 1996-1997. In *Prisoners of Hope,* he offered this statement:

> During WWII, U.S. troops were the best equipped fighting men in the world. But the one vital element that enabled me to survive the war and my POW experience was not GI issue. It was supplied by my father and mother. It was portable, took no space in my barracks bag, and, being invisible, could not be confiscated by the enemy. It was my faith—my Christian upbringing. My faith became a mighty bulwark against the brutality, cold, hunger, forced marches, boxcar rides, and bombing I endured. Faith became my constant companion, my comfort against the inhumanity of my enemy. I did not have to return it to the quartermaster when I was discharged. I brought it back home with me and relied on it to help raise my family, run a successful busi-

ness, and return to society some of the good fortune that has come my way through faith.

Philippians 4:19

But my God shall supply all your need according to his riches in glory by Christ Jesus.

1st Battalion, 1st Regiment, 1st Marines (Unauthorized) Pocket Patch

The 1st Battalion 1st Marines is an infantry battalion in the United States Marine Corps based at Camp Pendleton, California. The unit is nicknamed the "First of the First" and has the motto "Ready to fight." The First Marines have served in combat in WWII, Korea, Vietnam, Desert Storm, Operation Enduring Freedom, and Operation Iraqi Freedom.

Everett Pope served with the 1st Battalion of the 1st Marines during WWII and received the Medal of Honor for action on Peleliu Island. He offered the following advice for life in *VALOR*.

When I speak to young people, I often suggest to them that real courage is in doing the right thing. We all know what is right. We learn this at home, in church, and at school—but it frequently takes much courage to do what we know is right!

Thomas Kelley served with the River Assault Division 152 during the Vietnam War. He also received the Medal of Honor and offered a similar sentiment in *VALOR:* "Knowing the right thing to do is usually easy. Doing the right thing is often very tough."

We walk by faith, not by sight (II Corinthians 5:7).

Knowing what's right and doing what's right are often directly related to faith. There is no substitute for this knowledge. Faith offers hope, and it is an amazing source of strength to do what is right, not what is wrong.

Hebrews 11:1

Now faith is the substance of things hoped for, the evidence of things not seen.

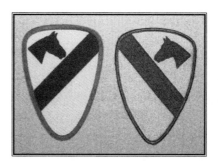

1st Cavalry Division
Right (Combat) and Left Shoulder Sleeve Insignia

The Army has used shoulder sleeve insignia on dress and field uniforms since WWI. These insignia indicate a specific military unit. The patch or insignia worn on the left shoulder indicates the current unit of assignment. A patch or insignia worn on the right shoulder indicates service with a unit during combat and is often referred to as a "combat patch." Interestingly, a few right shoulder sleeve combat patches are mirror images of the left shoulder patch. An example of this is the 1st Cavalry Division combat patch. The reasoning for the mirror image is so the head of the horse faces forward in the direction of battle and is advancing forward rather than facing rearward, suggesting retreat.

In *Prisoners of Hope*, retired Navy Captain Eugene "Red" McDaniel who was a POW in Vietnam for over six years, offered this wisdom, "Without battle, no man can come to victory; the greater the battle, the greater the victory."

In combat, both human and spiritual, we find great encouragement from Scripture. We read that "the battle, (the fight) belongs to the Lord" (II Chronicles 20:15b). And we also find comfort in knowing "the Lord will go before you, and the God of Israel will be your rear guard" (Isaiah 52:12).

II Timothy 4:7; Ephesians 6:12

I have fought a good fight, I have finished my course, and I have kept the faith.

For our fight (our battle) is not against flesh and blood, but against authorities and powers, against the world-rulers of this dark night, against the spirits of evil in the heavens.

Part 3

Life Stories

*CADUCEUS—Civil War Hospital Steward Sleeve Insignia
and WWI Bronze and Gold Collar Medical Corps Insignia*

The Army Medical Department of the U.S. Army was established as the "Army Hospital" in 1775. In 1851, a caduceus was embroidered in yellow on green silk and was worn as the insignia for hospital stewards of the Medical Department. The caduceus insignia was approved for wear in 1902 for officer and enlisted soldiers.

YOU'RE GOING TO BE A PHYSICIAN

I know the thoughts and plans I have for you, says the Lord (Jer. 29:11a).

As a senior in high school, I was considering joining the Navy after graduation. I was not a stellar student. When I describe my academic success to my children, I tell them I made the high school B honor roll twice by pure accident. As I reflect on my academic achievement to that point, I would best describe it in this way: I periodically failed to meet my lofty goal of academic mediocrity.

I excelled in athletics in high school, receiving varsity letters in football and track. I won the conference title in the 440 yard dash, held a few track and field records and was the captain of the track team. I guess you could have called me an athlete, but no one ever accused me of being an academic standout.

In the spring of my senior year, I attended a youth retreat with my church youth group at the Lake of the Ozarks. We spent the weekend at Windermere, a Southern Baptist church camp. On the final evening of the retreat, a missionary spoke to the group. We were sitting near the shoreline of the lake. Someone had started a bonfire. We watched the fire burn and listened to the speaker as he told us, "God has a plan and a purpose for your life." That was the first time that I remember anyone ever saying that God had a plan for my life.

The missionary then said, "Maybe God will tell you tonight what he has planned for your life, what He wants you to do. If He does, I would like for you to come down by the bonfire and tell me." I listened to the words, waiting only for the service to end so I could head back to my room and fool around with my friends. I could have never imagined what would happen next!

The young fellow standing beside me started to make his way past me and head toward the missionary and the bonfire. I grabbed his elbow and asked, "What are you doing? Where are you going?" He responded, "God just told me that I am going to be a pastor!" I couldn't believe it! It seemed so strange to think that God has a plan for our life, and He had told the young man beside me His plan. Talk about weird!

I watched as my friend made his way to the missionary and began to speak with him. Behind me, I heard a voice say, "You're going to be a physician." I didn't pay attention to the voice. I assumed someone behind me was talking about becoming a doctor. I heard the voice again, "You're going to be a physician." Curious, I turned and looked to see who was talking, but there was nobody there. I thought to myself, *This is really strange! I heard the voice twice, but nobody is behind me. I am also sure there is no way that God is talking to me, and I am positive that there is absolutely no way that He is going to use me as a physician! God knows, my teachers know, and I know that I am not a scholar!*

As I stood and wondered about the statement, I heard the voice again: "You're going to be a physician." Amazed, I then knew God was speaking to me. However, I was also pretty sure He didn't know what He was talking about, but I headed toward the bonfire and told the missionary God said that I was going to be a physician.

The human lesson and reality is that in life you may believe or even be convinced that you do not have the ability to accomplish much. With faith, hard work, and God's help, you can accomplish more than you ever thought possible. There is an old adage: "With the help of God, I cannot fail. Without God, I cannot succeed."

The scriptural reference is in I Samuel 3:10 where Samuel responded to the third call from God by saying, "Speak, for thy servant hears." I would like to encourage you to listen for the voice of God—He has a plan for your life! In my life, I have lived the scripture found in 1 Corinthians 1:27, "God had chosen the foolish things of this world to confound the wise."

WWII and (unauthorized) Korean War
40th Infantry Division Shoulder Sleeve Insignia

The 40th Infantry Division is a unit with the California Army National Guard. It is sometimes called the "Sunshine Division" and has served in combat in WWI, WWII, the Korean War, the War in Kosovo, and also in the Global War on terrorism.

WHY ME?

He causes his sun to rise on the evil and the good and sends rain on the righteous and the unrighteous (Matt. 5:45b).

At some point during my medical student career, I started smoking and drinking coffee. I concluded that smoking cigarettes and drinking coffee would help me stay awake during the long hours of study. In high school, athletics and good health were an important part of my life, and I must also admit that I had never spent many nights studying in high school so I had never before felt the need to smoke or drink coffee.

The coffee and tobacco helped pass the time during the long hours of study in the late nights and early mornings. I continued these habits through my internship and residency. In 1977, while brushing my teeth, I noticed a slightly tender, irregular, grey lesion on the side of my tongue. I made an appointment with the ENT department at the University. A biopsy was scheduled and performed; the diagnosis, leukoplakia, was considered to be a precancerous lesion. After the biopsy, the lesion disappeared.

I didn't pay much attention to the diagnosis since the lesion went away. I continued on with my life and made no change in my coffee and tobacco habits. Over the years, I had also wandered away from my faith in God, and it seemed most of the life decisions I made were the wrong ones.

In 1979, I was working in a private community hospital. I noticed another sore on my tongue in the same area. The lesion was mildly painful and ulcerated. I asked a friend who was a general surgeon at the hospital to look at the lesion. He felt I was too young to have a malignancy but recommended a biopsy anyway. The biopsy was performed, and we waited for the pathology report. He called me very early in the morning a few days later with the results—the diagnosis was cancer. He told me I needed to see an ENT surgeon as soon as I could because they might have to remove part or all of my tongue.

I will be quick to admit that when I heard the word "cancer," my tobacco habit ended immediately. After consultations with two ENT specialists, I elected to have surgery in St. Louis, preferring to be close to home. The surgery was considered a success. My speech was impaired for months but over time returned to normal.

By 1980, I had wandered so far from my faith and my spiritual moorings that my life was a wreck. I decided to return to the University and accepted a junior staff position, hoping to straighten out my life. In 1981, I met and started dating Vicki, a nurse who grew up on a farm in rural Minnesota. She was also divorced. Over time, we discussed marriage and set a date of July 4, 1982.

We were both concerned about our relationship failures and agreed that we would center our marriage around faith. We agreed that we would attend church together every Sunday morning and that the only time we would not be in church together was if we were on call or sick. With time, the happiness that had eluded us for so long seemed to be settling into our marriage.

In November 1982, I experienced a persistent sore throat.

Using a flashlight and looking into a mirror, I saw a round, ulcerated sore in my throat. Concerned, I told Vicki. A friend looked at the lesion and referred me to an oral surgeon. He performed a biopsy, and we waited anxiously for the results. I received a call from him on December 10th, Vicki's birthday. It was cancer—what a birthday present! I remember thinking, *Not now! I'm just beginning to straighten my life out. Why now? Why me?*

The surgery was performed in January 1983. We returned home believing all was well and trusting God for healing. Two weeks later we returned to St. Louis for a follow-up examination. The surgeon walked into the room. The expression on his face was somber. When he spoke, it was obvious he was trying to hold back tears. I still remember his words, "I have some bad news. We were unable to remove all of the tumor." Looking at Vicki, I recognized her pain as she began to cry. She asked, "What do we do next?"

The surgeon recommended radiation, believing it was the best treatment available to obtain a cure. I waited two weeks to allow some healing before I started radiation treatment and then traveled to St. Louis each day for six weeks of therapy.

By the time the therapy was complete, I was pretty miserable. The skin on my face was burned and discolored. My throat was painful and blistered, and food no longer had any taste. I had lost a considerable amount of weight during the treatment. After the therapy, I began to wonder what the future might hold.

Over the next few years, we began to distance our lives from our past mistakes and also the worry about malignant disease. Our marriage was growing stronger, we enjoyed our work, and in 1987, we experienced the blessing and joy of the birth of our son, Joshua. I seemed to be doing well, and my medical follow-up exams were all good. I was nearing the six-year point in time where I would be considered cured of cancer.

In 1988, I was re-assigned in the Army Reserves as a mobilization asset to the 1st Special Operations Command at Fort Bragg, North Carolina. In 1989, I had the opportunity to attend the Israeli paratrooper school at Tel Nof, Israel. While in Israel, I began to experience a sore throat, similar to the pain I had experienced in 1982.

With my return from Israel, I could see another grey ulcerated lesion. We scheduled another appointment and traveled to St. Louis. The surgeon looked at the lesion and immediately set up another biopsy with surgery to follow. The surgery removed not only the lesion but much of the surrounding soft tissue in my throat. It extended into my mouth and along my jaw, leaving the jawbone partially exposed. A plastic repair was scheduled to follow after partial healing of the wound. Two weeks later we returned to St. Louis to discuss the next step and received devastating news. Even with the extensive surgery, a residual tumor remained. I looked at Vicki, wondering in my mind what the future would hold for us and thought to myself, *Why me?*

We returned home and I spent a number of days making sure my personal and legal matters were in order in case there was to be no cure. We returned to the hospital, covered by the prayers of family, friends, and people across the nation. The surgical plan was to remove both abnormal and healthy tissue in my throat, mouth, tongue, and jaw, and extend the incision down into my neck to ensure there was no tumor there.

The surgery took more than ten hours. The early post-op days were miserable, and the physical and emotional adjustment to the disfiguration took months to reconcile. There was, however, one difference. After all the surgeries, radiation therapy, and the setbacks of the new and residual tumor, the question I asked was no longer, *Why me?* The thought, now more than a question, was, *Why not me?* I had learned to be content. My faith had reached the point where I was able to accept whatever God had planned for me.

I love the wisdom that Dave Roever shared in *A Gathering of Eagles*. In 1969, Dave was severely injured in combat in Vietnam. He sustained severe burns and massive injuries to almost his entire body. His advice is,

> Life is not fair, and all who live long enough to discover the reality of this truth also live long enough to discover that the really

big question of life is not, is it fair, but rather, how will one deal with life's inequities.

I speak to men's groups across the nation about leadership, success, significance, and faith. I periodically introduce myself with the statement, "I've had five biopsies, four major surgeries, and two months of radiation therapy over a ten-year period to make me this ugly—what's your excuse?"

When I speak to men's groups, I sometimes share my testimony of how I turned from faith and God. But God remained faithful, and during the difficult times, my faith was restored and became strong. God was able to use disease to get my attention, to turn my heart to love for and service to Him. At times I share the scriptural reference of Judges 15:5 saying, "Just as Samson used the jawbone of a jackass to get the attention of the Philistines, God used the jawbone of a jackass to get my attention." The real question in life is not, *Why me?* Rather it is, *Why not me?*

WWII and Current Missouri Army National Guard
Shoulder Sleeve Insignia

The Missouri Army National Guard is a component of the United States Army and was originally formed in 1890. The Militia Act of 1903 organized various state militias into the current National Guard system. Army Guard units comprise almost half of the US Army's available combat forces and one-third of its support units.

STAY IN THE LAND

They said, Turn ye again now every one from his evil way, and from the evil of your doings, and dwell in the land that the Lord hath given unto you and to your fathers for ever and ever (Jeremiah 25:5).

In 1988, my pastor challenged the membership of the church to read *The One Year Bible* (TOYB). I was one of about 10-12 individuals who agreed to the challenge and commitment. I was already in the habit of reading from the New Testament almost every day, but I had never read the entire Bible cover to cover.

My father was a wonderful example and moral compass. I watched him read the Bible every day. Because of his example and the request of my pastor, I began reading TOYB in January 1989. During that year, I carried the Bible with me to Israel where I attended the Israeli paratrooper school, to Mexico, and then to Panama and Peru. After completing TOYB the first year, I decided to read it again and have been doing so ever since.

The cover of my *One Year Bible* is faded, worn, and now partially covered with plastic and duct tape. All of the pages are dog eared. After more than twenty years of study, almost every page has passages that are underlined and highlighted with comments and life events noted in the margins. This Bible is well-traveled...I have carried it to many nations of the world.

In 1999, my job at the hospital became very difficult. One of the three staff physicians in the department moved to the University, due in part to a significant salary disparity between the University and the VA. The chief of the department also turned in his retirement paperwork, leaving only me to do the work of three physicians. To complicate the situation, I learned about a similar VA position in Arkansas that offered a greater salary. Although I felt a deep loyalty to the veteran patients in Columbia, I decided to look at the Arkansas position.

My wife, Vicki, and I had significant reservations about moving. Vicki's three greatest concerns were: leaving Columbia and the farm she loved; leaving close friends and a wonderful church family; and her greatest concern, finding the right Christian school for our son, Josh. From the very beginning, she told me she was willing to do whatever I needed to do, but her heart grieved at the thought of moving.

We took a weekend trip and traveled to visit the hospital. Our first stop was at a Christian school—what an amazing place! The students were friendly and seemed happy, and the academic and athletic programs were excellent. Walking away from the school, Vicki felt an immediate release, a burden lifted. Her prayers answered, the concern and the worry were now part of the past. The school was more than we could have hoped for.

We then visited the VA, had lunch with the Director and staff, and spent the weekend visiting a church and looking at homes and the town. It seemed like the possibility of a move might be a good fit for me and for the family. To make the offer even more attractive, the VA would pay for our move and even purchase our home if we were unable to sell it. I was offered the position of Chief of the department with a significant increase in salary.

We returned home and immediately began to seek the will of God for our lives. We prayed, we fasted, and we sought God's direction in His Word. We also asked friends and church family to pray for direction and help to make the right decision. The Director of the hospital asked that I make a decision by October 15th.

After work on the evening of October 14th (coincidently, my mother's birthday), I started my daily reading in TOYB. The reading began in Jeremiah, the 2nd through the 25th chapters. When I read Jeremiah 25:5, I stopped. I read the verse again and then again. The verse read, "Dwell in the land that the Lord hath given you and to your fathers forever and ever." I had read that same chapter and verse on my mother's birthday for ten years, but now, in 1999, that verse had a much deeper and more personal meaning.

The next morning I called the Director of the hospital in Arkansas and declined the position. I went to the Director and Chief-of-Staff of the hospital in Columbia and told them I was not going to move. I also informed them that the University had offered me a job, but I would prefer to remain at the VA. I was asked to stay and was offered the identical salary of the VA we had visited. The Director and the Chief-of-Staff also made a commitment to fill the open staff physician positions in the department.

As I look at the importance of knowledge and wisdom, I am reminded of the wonderful advice for life by General Lloyd "Fig" Newton in *A Gathering of Eagles*. The advice: "Always strive to learn something new. If we are not learning something new each day, we should consider it an incomplete day."

Spiritually, as I reflect on the importance of studying the Word and learning something new every day, I am reminded that God speaks to us when we read His Word. There are times when the Scriptures will help us make a decision that will keep us in the will and plan of God.

Do you read the Bible every day? Would you consider reading *The One Year Bible*? God might have a passage for you that will change your life!

> *For the word of God is quick and powerful and sharper than any two-edged sword, piercing even to the dividing asunder of soul and spirit, and is a discerner of the thoughts and intents of our heart* (Heb. 4:12).

In Psalm 119:105, we read, "Thy word is a lamp unto my feet, and a light unto my path." On October 14, 1999 reading from my *One Year Bible*, the Word of God was a light to my path and helped direct me along the path of life.

USAF and USN Flight Suit Patches for 100 Landings

The rank of Centurion does not exist in the American military. In Imperial Rome, the rank of Centurion was given to a soldier who commanded a centuria or century. The true number of individuals in a centuria can vary but most military historians agree that Centurions commanded between 60 to 80 men and at times as many as 100 soldiers.

THE CENTURION

When Jesus heard these things, he marvelled at him, and turned him about, and said unto the people that followed him, I say unto you, I have not found so great faith, no, not in Israel (Luke 7:9).

I awoke early and made my way to the bow of the small Peruvian Naval vessel. It was the fifth day of a three week military humanitarian medical mission. We were seeing patients in villages along the Amazon River. We left San Palo, Peru, very early that morning, Sunday, December 10, 1989—my wife's birthday. Another birthday away from home and family. Birthdays are important, especially to my wife. It seemed the Army frequently arranged for me to be away from home on that day.

I was blue as I thought about her and my family. To lift my spirits, I decided to have my own Sunday church service. Opening my small pocket New Testament, I turned to one of my favorite passages, the seventh chapter of Luke. I read once again the familiar story of the centurion who asked Christ to heal his servant. Christ spoke of the centurion's faith, saying, "I have not found such great faith, no, not in Israel." Once again I was encouraged by the story of a soldier with great faith. As we traveled along the Amazon, I read the remainder of the chapter and reflected on the story of the widow of Nain and how Christ raised her son from the dead, returning him alive to his mother. I had no idea that a similar story would evolve that same day.

The trip from San Palo was long, and we arrived at dusk at the small village of Triumfo. A family rushed up with their young son who was extremely sick. He had been vomiting and had had diarrhea for many days. As I pinched the skin on his abdomen, it remained raised in an elevated mound. In the normal individual, the elasticity of the skin will allow it to rebound and quickly flatten. My fear and suspicion of profound dehydration was confirmed.

There were four military physicians in our group—myself, one other American, and two Peruvians. As we looked at the small boy, we realized he was extremely sick and that the prognosis was grave. We discussed the problem and the possible solutions with the family. We knew the child would not survive without intensive medical intervention, but no local medical care was available.

The medical supplies we had on board the vessel were very limited, so we decided to take the sick child and his family to a small, but primitive, Peruvian hospital about four hours downriver. We only had a few IV solutions and some IV tubing and needles. The youngster was so sick and his dehydration so severe that he was almost unresponsive. As we started down the river, the two Peruvian physicians tried to start an IV on the child. After many unsuccessful attempts, they asked the other American physician to try. Despite numerous attempts, he too was unable to start an IV.

We discussed other options, but we were limited by our lack of more appropriate medical supplies. The atmosphere was extremely tense in the crowded cabin room on the small vessel. The room was dimly lit, hot, and muggy. The smell of diesel fuel, sweaty uniforms, and body odor was thick in the air. The child's family—his mother, father and two siblings—watched with wide eyes as we tried and tried again to start IV fluids without success. As each minute passed, the child seemed less responsive even to the painful needle sticks. He was moving closer to death.

As his pulse weakened and his rapid heart rate became faint, I lifted his eyelids and saw that his eyes were rolled back in his head and his pupils appeared dilated. We were weary from the long day, but there would be no rest. We knew if we did not get fluid into the child, he would die.

The two Peruvian physicians re-examined the child and agreed with us that death was imminent. They proceeded to inform the family that we were unable to save the child. The mother began to quietly sob as did the boy's siblings as they surrounded the dying child. The father sat quietly watching. Looking at his face, you could see the pain and tell that his heart was breaking. The other American physician headed for the door, trying to hide his tears and silence his own grief.

The youngster's vascular system was collapsing. There seemed to be no vein available that we could use. The thought came to me that if I could just get a needle into the faint and barely palpable femoral artery near the groin that maybe there might be a slim chance of saving him.

As I felt for the pulse of the femoral artery, I began to recite to myself Psalm 91, the soldier's Psalm: "He that dwells in the secret place of the most High shall abide under the shadow of the Almighty. I will say of the Lord, He is my refuge and my fortress: my God, in Him will I trust." As I finished the verse, I stuck the needle once again into the almost lifeless child. Arterial flow! It worked, praise God!

We compressed the IV bag and began administrating fluids. It was a tiny victory, but the situation remained extremely grave. As we continued down river, we realized that without a miracle we would not arrive at the small hospital in time to save the child. Even if we did get there, and if he were still alive, there was still a good chance he might not survive.

After an hour passed, the arterial line stopped flowing; it wasn't working. Once again I searched for a vein to use. I noticed a small one above the child's ear. Again I prayed the words in Psalm 91 and was able to start an IV. I was relieved but still very concerned. By this time the family, the physicians, and the medics were all physically and emotionally exhausted.

After midnight, we finally reached the small village and began our trip carrying the child on winding, narrow paths through the dark jungle to the hospital. On the way, the IV line was accidently pulled out, and our hopes for continued fluid replacement were dashed again. When we arrived, the caretaker told us that a part-time physician and nurse staffed the hospital, but they would not return until the morning.

We gently placed the child on one of the few beds. With another prayer, I was able to start another IV by the light of a flashlight held by one of our group. We left the boy and his family and one of our medics. At that point, there was nothing more that we could do for the boy. We left him in the hospital and headed back through the hot, sticky darkness of the jungle.

When I climbed into my bunk, I thought about home, my wife and her birthday, and my young son who was about the same age as the child we desperately tried to save. Exhausted, I was finally able to sleep.

When I awoke, the other American physician came by and told me the news. He had returned to the hospital early in the morning to check on the boy before we headed down the river again. He told me that not only was the child alive, he was awake in his mother's arms, talking, and drinking fluids! He was alive!

God does indeed work in mysterious ways. He brought four physicians together—two from Peru and two from America—to meet a family with a dying child on the Amazon river. The physicians worked all night to save the child, finally reaching a small hospital that the family would have never been able to get to since they had no boat. When it still seemed hopeless, God intervened to accomplish what seemed impossible. Miracles do indeed happen today, even on the Amazon River.

When I arrived home, I greeted my wife and son. I sat down with my wife and I told her, "I'm sorry I was away on your birthday, but I need to tell you a Happy Birthday story." I explained, "Because I was away from home on your birthday, a little boy is alive in Peru." Obviously God had a plan. He set up the time and the place for those people to all come together so the life of one child would be saved. I don't know what plan God has for this child, but I'm sure it must be special!

WWII 777th Tank Battalion Shoulder Sleeve Insignia

The 777th (TD-Tank Destroyer) Tank Battalion served in combat in Europe for a short period between February and May of 1945 near the end of WWII. The unit was sometimes referred to as the "Lucky Triple Seven."

MEN WITHOUT FEAR

Judges 7:7—the 7th book, the 7th chapter, the 7th verse:

And the Lord said unto Gideon, By the three hundred men...

During the Persian Gulf War, I served with the 3rd Group Army Special Forces (Airborne). In preparation for the ground war, and as one of the soldiers selected to go forward with the ground invasion into Kuwait City, I was required to meet with a member of our intelligence section. One of the possibilities discussed was what could happen if we were captured and held as an Iraqi prisoner-of-war. We were asked a myriad of questions. It was believed our answers could be used by those who would be involved in a rescue attempt. One scenario discussed was our identification if a rescue attempt was made after many years of captivity.

During the extensive interview we were asked many questions. Our responses were written down and entered into our record.

These questions and our answers could be used to ensure our correct identification by those who would attempt to rescue us. I remember one question vividly because of my answer. The question was, "What number would I give to those who, during a rescue attempt, would ask for my identification number?" We were instructed not to use birthdays, anniversaries, phone numbers, or ID numbers because the enemy might have access to those numbers.

I decided on the number 777. My reasoning was spiritual. Many Bible scholars believe the number 7 to be an important number because of its use in the Bible. I felt the number 777 would be easy to remember because I would remember the number 7 for God the Father, the next 7 as God the Son, and the last 7 as God the Holy Spirit.

At the end of the interview I remember my disbelief when I was informed that if I were not recognized by those who were sent to rescue me and unable to answer their questions, then I would be left behind. I remember asking, "You mean you would really leave me behind?" The response was, "Yes, you will be given two choices. One is, we will leave you. I asked, "What is the second choice?" The response was, "Do you really want me to answer that question?"

Biblical Reference

With my return home from the Gulf, my already established faith began to increase. I began to make a conscious effort to seek God daily and made a decision to live a life dedicated to Him. During one of my daily times of Bible study, I remembered my 777 answer. I began to search the Bible for the number 777. The only mention of the number 777 was that Noah's father lived to be seven hundred and seventy-seven years old. After a few weeks of trying to determine if there was any biblical significance to the number, I awoke one morning with the thought...look in the Bible at the 7th book, the 7th chapter and the 7th verse.

I turned to Judges, the 7th book in the Bible, then to the 7th chapter and read the 7th verse. "And the Lord said unto Gideon, by the three hundred men that lapped will I save you and deliver the Midianites into your hand..."

I realized the passage was a war story, and I began to read and re-read the story over and over. After studying the passage I realized a truth that is relevant even today.

Let me quickly review the story with you. Verse 2 reads, "The Lord said the people are too many, lest Israel will say my own hand hath saved me." In verse 3, God told Gideon to "Proclaim whoever is fearful let him return." Twenty-two thousand returned, only ten thousand remained. I concluded that two-thirds of the men were fearful. This meant that only one-third were MEN WITHOUT FEAR. In verse 4, the Lord said, "The people are yet too many; bring them down to the water." There were 10,000 men without fear, but God would only use 300 men to fulfill His plan.

In verse 5, the Lord said, "Everyone that lappeth of the water, set by himself; likewise everyone that bows down to drink." Verse 6 tells us about 300 men who, while standing, lapped water with their hand to their mouth." The rest bowed down.

Although 9,700 were MEN WITHOUT FEAR, they bowed down to drink. Only 300 remained erect to drink. In my opinion, these men remained upright, looking for the enemy. They were prepared for battle. In verse 7, the Lord said, "By these 300 hundred men will I save you."

Relevance for Today

As I studied the passage, reading it over and over; I tried to determine its relevance for today. I came to the realization that even today, God continues to use only a small number of men and women. He uses a similar plan, a similar equation, spiritually speaking. In my experience, about one-third of men and women seem to be MEN and WOMEN WITHOUT FEAR—they are the individuals who are really seeking to be used by God. These are the men and women who have decided to follow God. However, God will only use a very small number of people to fulfill His divine plan.

How Can I Be Used by God?

How does God determine and then select these individuals? God will only use a few individuals to fulfill His divine plan because He does not intend for man to receive the glory for His plan or for what He is doing. I believe God separated His people by those who WITHOUT FEAR are WILLING, SEEKING, PREPARED, and COMMITTED to be used by God, and most importantly, are WILLING TO GIVE GOD THE GLORY for the victory.

The Spiritual Equation would look like this:

$$\frac{W + S + P + C}{gGg} = GDP$$

$$\frac{\text{Willing + Seeking + Prepared + Committed}}{\text{give God the glory}} = \text{God's Divine Plan}$$

You might ask the question. "How can I become one of the few who are really used by God to fulfill His divine plan?" I believe that you have to be IN THE WORD every day. Second, you have to be IN PRAYER every day, and third you must FREQUENTLY MEET with others of a like heart, mind, soul, and purpose. This will help you to be PREPARED to be used by God! Finally you must be willing to GIVE GOD THE GLORY for what He is doing, what he has done, and what He is going to do!

Chaplain Corps Badges
Spanish American War Chaplain Shoulder Strap
Current Army, Navy and Air Force Insignia

WE WILL SERVE THE LORD

And if it seem evil unto you to serve the Lord, choose you this day whom you will serve; whether the gods which your fathers served that were on the other side of the flood, or the gods of the Amorites, in whose land ye dwell; but as for me and my house, we will serve the Lord.

The above verse in Joshua 24:15 is my favorite Bible verse because it is my prayer for my children, their children, their children, their children, and all who follow after them, that they will serve the Lord.

Desmond Doss received the Medal of Honor in WWII, serving as a medic with the 77th Infantry Division in the Pacific. Desmond was a dedicated man of faith. As a non-combatant, he never carried or even touched a weapon, yet he saved the lives of countless soldiers. He is credited with saving seventy-five men on the Maeda escarpment on Okinawa. On the back of his Medal of Honor card, you will find the Scripture, Proverbs 3:5-6; "Trust in the Lord with all thy heart; and lean not unto thine own understanding. In all thy ways acknowledge him, and he will direct thy path."

Rudy Hernandez received the Medal of Honor serving as an infantryman with the 187th Regimental Combat Team in Korea. Rudy was severely wounded protecting the lives of fellow soldiers. On the back of his Medal of Honor card, you will find the Scripture, Roman 1:16; "For I am not ashamed of the gospel of Jesus Christ."

These men offered their "advice for life" in both *VALOR* and *A Gathering of Eagles*. I was so impressed with the courage and humility of these men that I decided to place Scriptures on the back of my business card. The first Scripture, my favorite, is Joshua 24:15.

I once had a medical student stop by who was also a commissioned officer as well as a West Point graduate. He was seeking advice about a career path in medicine, the military, and faith. One of his questions was, "How do you share your faith with others in your medical practice and in the military?" I pulled a business card from my pocket and handed it to him, asking him to look at the back of the card and said, "Let me tell you a story…"

A number of years ago I wrote several articles for the *Journal of Military Medicine* about combat trauma. Most of the articles were case reports. In 1990, I evaluated a number of x-ray examinations on a veteran who had one of his legs amputated twenty years after he was wounded in Vietnam. The amputation was due to complications of chronic osteomyelitis, a chronic bone infection, complicated by cancer in the old wound.

The case was unusual so I decided to contact the patient to see if he would be willing to let me use his exams and story in one of the articles. Over time, I misplaced his contact information. About fifteen months after I saw the patient's x-rays, the forgotten contact information surfaced on my desk from its place below the piles of "need-to-do" notes. Remembering the case, I decided to call him.

I called his home and his wife answered. I explained who I was and why I was calling and asked to speak to her husband. Her response was, "He is an inpatient in the hospital right now…If you go to his room, I'm sure he will talk with you." I thought, *Wow, what a coincidence!*

I headed to his room thinking about the coincidence that he would be a patient in the hospital on the very day that I called to see if he would let me write his story. When I arrived at his room, I introduced myself, handed him my business card, and explained why I was there. I then asked him if he would be willing to let me write a case report for the combat trauma series about his injuries. He listened to my request and after a few moments, responded. "Yes, you can write about my case, but there is one thing I want you to do for me. I have one favor to ask before I will allow you to write the story." When I heard the statement, I wondered if he wanted to be paid for being included in the series.

With some trepidation I responded, "I will try. What is the favor?"

"I want you to find the doctor that took care of me in Vietnam," he said, "the physician that saved me from having my legs amputated. I was never able to thank him for saving my legs, and I want to thank him."

I thought about the impossibility of his request. How do you find a physician twenty years after he took care of a patient in Vietnam? I asked, "Do you know his name and where he was from?" He responded, "I don't know his first name, and I'm not sure how to spell his last name; but he was an Army Captain and he had a southern accent." I wrote down the last name he gave me, thinking to myself, *There is no way I will ever find this guy!*

I returned to my office, wondering how many physicians had been in Vietnam and how many thousands of injured patients were treated. I concluded that this could be a very interesting article, but it would never get written, let alone published.

As I thought about how I could locate the physician, I decided to call the American College of Surgeons (ACS) and ask if they might be able to locate an orthopedic surgeon with the possibility of an incorrectly spelled last name. I called information and found the ACS telephone number. I then called their office, explained my dilemma, and requested their help. The secretary pulled up the computerized registry and responded, "There is no orthopedic surgeon with a name similar to the name you have." I thanked her for her efforts and hung up the phone.

I wondered if the spelling of the name was incorrect or if the physician had stopped practicing medicine. Was he even a member of the ACS or was he still living? After a period of time, I decided to call the office again and ask if they had any surgeon in any specialty with a name similar to the name I was given. When I reached the office, I apologized to the secretary, asking if she would be willing to do one more search before I gave up. She agreed and opened the alphabetical membership list. After a few minutes she responded, "There is one physician with a name similar to the name you are looking for. The name is spelled differently and I doubt that it is him because he is a neurosurgeon. He does, however, live in the south." She gave me the office number; I wrote it down and immediately called the doctor's office.

When the receptionist answered the phone, I explained why I was calling. She told me that the doctor was out of the office, but maybe I could reach him at home. When I called the home, the doctor's wife answered and, once again, I explained why I was calling. She told me that her husband had served in Vietnam, but she did not know where or with what unit. She asked for my phone number and said she would give the message to her husband when he arrived home.

It was the end of the workday so I headed for home. Later that evening I received a call from the physician. I explained why I had called and asked if he was ever involved in the care of a soldier in Vietnam who had sustained severe bilateral lower extremity injuries. I asked if he was the physician that made the decision not to amputate the legs of the young soldier while two other physicians believed that they should amputate both legs. He hesitated for a moment, and then responded, "Yes, I'm the guy."

I related the complete story and my reason for trying to contact him. I also told him that the veteran had always wanted to thank him for saving his legs and asked if he would be willing to speak with the veteran. I waited, hearing no response but the sound of muffled crying. He finally responded, "Yes, please call me tomorrow at my office." Excited, I hung the phone up in disbelief. I could not believe my good luck! In less than a day I had found the doctor, and he was willing to speak with the veteran. It was more than obvious that more than good luck was involved.

The next morning I visited the patient and told him that I had found the doctor and that he would be able to talk to him later that morning. The patient came to my office in a wheelchair, I placed the call, the physician answered, and I handed the phone to the veteran. As he said hello, I left the office to give him some privacy, but I could hear both men crying, trying to talk over sobs and tears.

Two weeks after this episode, a man stopped me in the hall of the hospital as I was getting on an elevator. He said, "You don't know me, but I want to thank you." I asked, "Have we met?" He told me he had been the roommate of the patient who I interviewed about the article. He further explained that he wanted to thank me because he was able to share his faith with the patient. Apparently, the evening I first visited the patient, the patient noticed the Scriptures on the back of my business card. The patient then showed the card to his roommate, asking, "Will you help me find these verses in the Bible?"

The man then told me, "Because of the Scriptures on your card, I was able to share the gospel of Jesus Christ with someone. I just wanted to tell you the story and to thank you." He then said, "Before I came to the hospital, I prayed that I might have an opportunity to share my faith with someone. I wanted you to know the rest of the story." God sometimes works in mysterious ways... "As for me and my house, we will serve the Lord."

Fire and Rescue, Police and Sheriff Department
Shoulder Sleeve Insignia

When we think about service to the nation, we commonly think about those serving in the military. There are, however, literally hundreds of thousands of individuals who serve the nation in uniform. They live and serve in almost every community in law enforcement and in fire and rescue departments. Many work in jobs that place them at great risk. There are currently more than three million individuals serving in the military, law enforcement, fire departments and rescue departments in America.

THOSE WHO SERVE

For a day in thy courts is better than a thousand. I had rather be a doorkeeper in the house of my God, than to dwell in the tents of wickedness (Ps. 84:10).

The fabric of my life is woven with the thread of the love of God, love of family, and love of nation. My two brothers and I served in Army uniform for a combined total of 93 years. My great-grandfather served as a soldier in the Civil War; our family served in the militia in the Colonial Wars, in the Revolutionary War, and in the War of 1812.

When I think of service to nation and the real cost of freedom, I am reminded of the quote by Gary Beikirch in *VALOR*. Gary received the Medal of Honor in Vietnam. He writes, "To really live, you must almost die. To those who fight for it, life and freedom have a meaning the protected will never know."

Freedom, both human and spiritual, has a great cost. That cost is paid in blood, sweat, tears, sacrifice, and death. The American Ex-POW association motto reminds us, "Freedom is not free!"

Cordino Longiotti is a WWII veteran and Ex-POW. In *PRISONERS OF HOPE*, he said, "Dying for freedom is not the worst thing that could happen; dying for freedom and being forgotten is."

Fred Ferguson received the Medal of Honor in Vietnam. When he speaks to students about freedom, he will often share the poem entitled, *It Has Always Been the Soldier.*

It is the soldier, not the reporter,
Who has given us freedom of the press;

It is the soldier, not the poet,
Who has given us freedom of speech;
It is the soldier, not the campus organizer,
Who has given us freedom to demonstrate;
It is the soldier
Who salutes the flag,
Who serves beneath the flag,
And whose coffin is draped by the flag.

I have a deep love and respect for those who currently serve, their families, and those who have already served. There are literally thousands of men and women serving in the armed forces, law enforcement, and fire and rescue units across this nation. For those who serve the nation in uniform, the words service, selfless-service, sacrifice, and suffering have a significant and personal meaning.

In *A Gathering of Eagles*, the following individuals offer their advice about service and leadership:

LTG Howard Graves, USA, (Ret) former Superintendent of West Point, states, "Leaders must have integrity because we are in positions of trust. It is important that we have a sincere concern for our fellow men and women because, frankly, we are not here for ourselves, as individuals or institutions. We are here for a greater cause—to glorify God and serve others."

MajGen John Grinalds, USMC, (Ret) and past President of the Citadel, offered this advice: "Lead through service to your troops, as Jesus led through service to us, even unto death."

Former Governor of Arkansas, Mike Huckabee, offered this statement: "The ultimate evaluation of effective leadership is not determined by how many people serve us, but rather how many people we serve."

Bill Bright, the late Founder of Campus Crusade for Christ, said, "Our Lord gave one major prerequisite to leadership—servanthood."

In Matthew 20:26-27, we read,

Whoever wants to become great among you must be your servant.
The Son of man came not to be served, but to serve, and to give his
life as a ransom for many.

During my military career, I spent many early morning hours
running in formation with Airborne soldiers. During these morning
runs, cadence was frequently called. Usually a non-commissioned
officer (NCO) calls a line of a cadence, and the soldiers repeat the
same line, singing in unison. I still remember one cadence. I periodically use it to illustrate love of God, love of family, and love of nation. The cadence is as follows:

C-130

C-130 rollin' down the strip,
Airborne daddy gonna take a little trip.
Stand up, hook up, shuffle to the door,
Jump right out and count to four.
Now if that main don't open wide,
I've got a reserve by my side.
If that one should fail me too,
Look out ground, I'm comin' on through.
If I die in a combat zone,
Box me up and ship me home.
Tell my wife I done my best,
Pin silver wings on my son's chest.

To the soldier, the final lines of the cadence have a poignant
meaning. "If I die in a combat zone, box me up and ship me home.
Tell my wife I done my best. Pin silver wings on my son's chest."

I know of no other group that has a greater love of home, a
greater love of spouse, and a greater love of children than those who
serve in uniform in harm's way.

When I speak to men's groups and at patriotic events, I periodically ask those present to follow me in the cadence. When we finish, I ask them to look at the last few lines from a human perspective, stressing the words home, wife, son. I then ask them to look at the same words from a spiritual perspective.

Spiritually, I look at home as heaven, my spouse and family as the family of God, and my son, my children, as my spiritual legacy. We need to ask ourselves, "Will anybody be in heaven because of us? Do we have a spiritual legacy? Will anybody be in heaven because of you?"

It was a great honor to serve the nation in uniform. I am proud of my service to this country and consider it a privilege to have served with elite Special Operations and Special Forces units.

Spiritually, I believe there is no greater honor than to serve God. In Psalm 84:10 we read, "I would rather be a doorkeeper in the house of God, than dwell in the tents of the wicked." For those who serve God, we would rather be a private in the Army of God than serve in the Army of the wicked.

*WWII First Special Service Forces
and Current Special Forces Shoulder Sleeve Insignia*

Special Forces units owe their legacy, heritage, and ancestry to the First Special Service Forces of WWII. My oldest brother served with the 5th Group Army Special Forces in Vietnam, and I served with the 3rd Group Army Special Forces during the Gulf War.

ROOTS—LEGACY, HERITAGE, AND ANCESTRY

During my post-graduate medical training and four-year residency at the University of Missouri, I developed an interest in learning about my family roots. In 1977, an extremely popular and now famous TV miniseries aired based on the book, *Roots*, by Alex Haley. The series was about slave families in early America and their ancestry. It stimulated an explosion in genealogical research across the nation.

After serving in the Maryland Militia during the Revolutionary War, John Coy Sr., and his son, John Coy Jr., and their families moved to Kentucky in the early 1790s. They settled there and lived near the small town of Hodgenville. (Interestingly, Hodgenville is the birthplace and boyhood home of President Abraham Lincoln.) My part of the Coy family moved to northern Missouri in 1855. I was curious if there might still be family in Kentucky.

Wanting to learn more about my Kentucky Coy family, I decided to make a trip to the Hodgenville area over a three-day weekend so I could look for family. It took a day to travel to Hodgenville. When I arrived in the town, I looked for a motel and searched for any Coy listed in the local phone book. I found one listing but decided not to call the number. I was a little apprehensive about what I might find and who I would meet. The next morning I asked for direction at a local gas station and headed off, looking forward to the adventure of meeting my Kentucky family.

I drove to the address, pulled into the drive, and got out. I walked to the front porch of the home and knocked on the door. I waited with both anticipation and excitement at this chance to meet family and discover more about my roots. The door slowly opened, and an elderly gentleman said, "Hello." As I looked at him, I was amazed. He looked like an identical twin to my uncle, Leon Coy. I was convinced we were related. To me it seemed obvious! I had found some of my Kentucky Coy family.

I introduced myself, told him why I was in Hodgenville, and

began to relate my family story. I explained that my family moved from Hodgenville to northern Missouri in the mid-1850s. Finishing the explanation and my story, I asked, "I was wondering if we might be related?"

Before I write his response, I need to share some additional information. The late 1970s was a different period of time...I guess they all are. The 70s were not as strange as the 60s, but the older generation still had difficulty relating to younger people. I guess it would be like my youngest son, Josh, showing up at the home of one of my conservative brothers, saying, "I like rap music. I wonder if we might be related?"

I appeared at the door of the Coy home wearing what was cool at that time—long sideburns, a turtle shell and turquoise beaded necklace, a silk long-sleeved shirt with a winged siren print pattern, and tan slacks that flared slightly at the cuff. After the question, "I was wondering if we might be related," Mr. Coy looked directly at me, then at my necklace, my shirt, and my slightly flared slacks. He looked me directly in the eyes and responded, "Nope."

He shut the door and walked away. I stood there wondering if I should attempt to explain the story once more. After I thought about it for a few moments, I realized there was no need to explain the story again—once a Coy makes up his mind, there is no reason to attempt any further discussion. The situation reminded me of the old adage, "Don't try to confuse me with the facts!" I turned, went to the car, and drove back to Missouri.

Spiritual Ancestry

We are frequently reminded of our spiritual roots and our connection to God in both the Old and the New Testaments of the Bible. Ancestry and legacy are central to our relationship with God and His Son, Jesus Christ. God wants us to understand the relationship He has with us and how we are related to Him and His Son.

In Genesis 25:32, we find the story of two brothers, Jacob and Esau, the oldest. Esau said to Jacob, "What good is the birthright for me?" He then sold his birthright to Jacob for a bowl of lentil soup...(He literally sold his birthright for a bowl of beans—ABOB.)

In life, the reality is that we often don't appreciate and even take for granted our human and our spiritual birthright. It is essential that we make the commitment and the concentrated effort to maintain our relationship with our human and spiritual family.

Ultimately, anything that separates us from our spiritual roots and our spiritual family is sin. "For all have sinned and come short of the glory of God" (Rom. 3:23). Sin is nothing more than "A Bowl of Beans"—ABOB.

Everyone has the propensity to sin, and sin separates us from God and His Son. Make it your highest priority to always honor your birthright and maintain your spiritual relationship with God and His Son.

At some point in time, we will all stand at the edge of life and eternity. It will be absolutely essential for us to have developed a relationship with God and His Son. If we claim our spiritual birthright, we will hear the greeting, "Welcome home, good and faithful servant. Come on in, you are part of the family of God." Don't trade your place in eternity for ABOB. When you get to heaven, you don't want to hear, "Nope," when you ask God, "I was wondering if we might be related?"

Civil War Kepi Hat/Company Letter Insignia

The smallest fighting unit in the Infantry of the Union Army during the Civil War was the Company. On paper, Companies were usually made up of one hundred men and were usually commanded by a Captain. Companies were at times divided into smaller units but only for short periods of time. They combined to form Battalions, Battalions combined to form Regiments, Regiments combined to form Brigades, Brigades combined to form Divisions, and Divisions combined to form Corps. Ultimately, Corps combined to form Armies. Letters of the alphabet were used to designate companies such as "A," "B," and "C." The letter "J" was not used because when written it could be confused with the letter "I." Brass letters of the alphabet were pinned to the top of a Kepi hat to help with unit identification.

MATTHEW A TO Z + 2

A number of years ago during my daily Bible study, I decided that I wanted to better understand the life and teachings of Jesus Christ. With that decision, I began a daily study of the Gospel of Matthew. As I read the Gospel over and over, I began to underline words in each chapter that would correspond to the number of the chapter and to the letter of the alphabet. For example, chapter 1 would be A, and chapter 2 would correspond to B. After doing this for weeks and months, I realized this method could be used as a tool to learn the content of each chapter. I believe this approach can be a great learning tool for Bible students of any age. I also feel this is a wonderful teaching tool for parents, grandparents, and teachers to use to teach their children, grandchildren, and students.

In Psalm 119:11 we read, "Thy word have I hidden in my heart that I might not sin against thee." A great companion verse is Psalm 119:105: "Thy word is a lamp to my feet and a light to my path."

After I interviewed 119 Ex-POWs for the book, *Prisoners of Hope*, I was impacted by how much faith and the Word meant to those who experienced captivity, starvation, beatings, and torture.

Those who had a Bible or knew the Word were comforted and remained hopeful. During the Vietnam War, those who were shot down early were not allowed to have anything to read, let alone a Bible, for almost five years. Many of those Ex-POWs commented that having a Bible would have been a great comfort and source of hope. For those who had memorized Scripture, they had hidden the Word in their hearts, and it gave them that comfort and hope.

A few years ago I heard Dr. James Dobson in a radio interview with Chuck Colson. Dr. Dobson commented on the statement made by the president of a well-known seminary comparing seminary students today with students in the past. The comment was, "When students start seminary today, they don't know Scripture. Many don't even know the basic teachings of Jesus." The small book, *Matthew A to Z + 2*, makes it possible to learn and teach the life of Christ by using the alphabet and alliteration. Using the book and learning the concept will allow an individual to know and even review the life of Christ using this method.

In Malachi 4:6 we read, "He shall turn the heart of the fathers to the children and the heart of the children to their fathers, lest I come and smite the earth with a curse." I am more convinced than ever that we have to learn the life of Christ and teach our children about Christ, His life, and teachings. If we do not, we reap the curse prophesied by Malachi.

The ABCs of Matthew

1. (A) ANCESTRY from ABRAHAM to Jesus. The ANGEL APPEARED saying, "Don't be AFRAID," AND then ANNOUNCED His ARRIVAL saying, "His name will be Immanuel which means, God with us" (Mt. 1:23).

2. (B) The BABY BOY will BE BORN in BETHLEHEM (Mt. 2:5). The wise men, following a BRIGHT star and BEARING gifts, BOWED down and worshipped the BABY BOY. King Herod had the BABY BOYS in BETHLEHEM killed.

3. (C) John the Baptist CRIED, "CHANGE your heart, your CARDIAC CONDITION." Many CAME CONFESSING (Mt. 3:2). John said, "Do something to show that you have CHANGED." Jesus CAME to John to be baptized. When Jesus was baptized, the COMFORTER CAME down.

4. (D) The DEVIL in the DESERT said, "Turn these stones to bread" (Mt. 4:3). DON'T DENY yourself a DELECTABLE DIET. Jesus responded, "DEPART from me." DON'T DARE tempt DEITY. The people in DARKNESS saw a great light.

5. (E) The Beatitudes: EXCEPTIONAL, EXCELLENT and EXCITING ETHICS. Do not swear by heaven or EARTH. You are the salt of the .EARTH. Do not let your EYE or EXTREMITY lead you astray. You have heard it said, "Love your neighbor." I tell you, "Love EVEN your ENEMIES" (Mt. 5:44).

6. (F) The FATHER'S prayer. FATHER FORGIVE us. Keep us FROM temptation and FROM evil. Don't FRET and be FRANTIC about the FUTURE. FIRST seek His kingdom (Mt. 6:33). The FUTURE will take care of itself.

7. (G) GIVE and you will GET. GOD will always GIVE GOOD GIFTS to those who ask. The GOLDEN Rule (Mt. 7:12). Do to others the same that you would have them do to you. Build your house on the GRANITE rock.

8. (H) HE HEALED HANSON'S disease (leprosy), the Centurion's HORRIBLY HURTING servant, and Peter's mother-in-law with a HIGH fever. HE also HEALED many possessed by evil spirits, also known as HAINTS. HE sent the demons into the HERD of HAM, and the HOGS HEADED HEADLONG into the sea (Mt. 8:32).

9. (I) He healed the paralyzed INVALID and the woman with the ISSUE of blood. He INVITED Matthew, the INCOME tax collector, to follow Him. IT IS the INFIRMED, those who are ILL,

who need a doctor. I did not come to INVITE the righteous but the sinner (Mt. 9:13).

10. (J) JESUS sent them on a JOURNEY saying, "Don't take any silver or gold", nothing that JINGLES in your purse. JUST give a drink in my name. You won't JUST JABBER and JAW. The Holy Spirit will speak through you (Mt. 10:20). JESUS JOURNEYED to teach and preach in other towns.

11. (K) To enter the KINGDOM, you must KEEP the faith. Father, thank you for KEEPING this KNOWLEDGE from the clever and giving it to the KIDS. No one will KNOW the Son except the Father (Mt. 11:27).

12. (L) Jesus healed the man with the LAME hand (Mt. 12:13). Some asked, "Is it LEGAL to heal on the Sabbath?" He said, "If your LAMB fell in a ditch, you would LIFT it out. LISTEN and LEARN from the Son of man."

13. (M) The seed that fell in good soil MULTIPLIED MIGHTILY (Mt. 13:8). When a MAN has MUCH, MUCH MORE will be given unto him. MANY asked, "Where does he get this wisdom?" Isn't MARY his MOTHER?"

14. (N) There is NO NEED to send the crowd away. He then NOURISHED the crowd that NUMBERED 5,000. Later, Peter walked toward Jesus on the water. He became NERVOUS, lost his NERVE and began to sink (Mt. 14:30)

15. (O) The woman said, "Have pity ON me. My ONLY daughter is sick." Christ responded, "I was ONLY sent to the house of Israel." After she asked again, he then said, "OH woman, great is your faith. Your daughter is OKAY. She is healed." He fed the crowd of 4,000, and food was left OVER (Mt. 15:37).

16. (P) PETER, you are PETRA the rock. "On you I will build my church." What you PERMIT on earth will be PERMITTED in

heaven. What does it PROFIT a man to gain the world? What PRICE can a man PAY to PURCHASE back his soul? (Mt. 16:26)

17. (Q) The QUARTET went up the mountain. They heard a QUOTE from heaven. "This is my Son in whom I am well pleased" (Mt. 17:5). The disciples began to QUAKE and QUIVER with fear. Peter asked, "Do we pay our tax QUOTA?" Jesus said, "Take the QUARTER from the mouth of the fish to pay tax."

18. (R) "Who is REALLY the greatest in heaven?" He responded, "It is the man who can be as humble as a child who will REALLY be the greatest in heaven" (Mt. 18:4). He also said, "If a man has a hundred sheep and one RUNS away, won't he go out and ROUND up and RESCUE the ROAMING sheep?"

19. (S) Jesus SAID, "A man SHALL leave his parents and SHALL STICK like SUPER glue to his SPOUSE. Man SHALL not SEPARATE what God joined together" (Mt. 19:6). The SON of man SHALL SIT on His throne in heaven.

20. (T) The farmer hired men to TOIL in his field. When THOSE who TOILED all day received THEIR silver coin, THEY grumbled saying, "You TREATED THOSE who TOILED little the same as THOSE who TOILED all day" (Mt. 20:11-12).

21. (U) The disciples UNTIED the colt and He rode into Jerusalem UPON the colt. UPSET with the moneychangers in the temple, Jesus turned their tables UPSIDE down (Mt. 21:12). When he was hungry he said to the UNPRODUCTIVE fig tree, "Nothing will ever grow on you. You are UNFIT."

22. (V) The king said, "Throw this VAGRANT out. He is not dressed for the wedding!" Trying to trap him, they asked three VEXING questions. When they asked, "What is the VERY greatest commandment?" He responded, "Love God, and then love your neighbor" (Mt. 22:37-39).

23. (W) Every man WHO promotes himself WILL be humbled. WHOEVER is WILLING to be humble WILL find promotion. WOE unto you, scribes and Pharisees, hypocrites! "You are like WHITEWASHED tombs full of WICKEDNESS" (Mt. 23:27). You filter out the mosquito but you swallow the WHOLE camel.

24. (X) "You must eXPECT His return. The sun will be darkened just like it was X'ED out. He will send His angels with an eXTRA-loud trumpet call. The eXCELLENT servant will be found eXECUTING his duty" (Mt. 24:26).

25. (Y) "Whatever YOU did for the least of these, the YOUNGEST, YOU did for me (Mt. 25:40). Come take YOUR inheritance. Whatever YOU failed to do for the least of these, the YOUNGEST, YOU failed to do for me."

26. (Z) Peter and the two sons of ZEBEDEE went with Christ to the garden. Jesus asked them to pray, but they fell asleep taking some Z's. Judas arrived. Acting like a ZERO, he betrayed Jesus. Peter drew his sword and ZAPPED off the ear of the servant of the High Priest (Mt. 26:52).

27. (C2) CHRIST was CONDEMNED. The CROWD CRIED, "CRUCIFY him" (Mt 27:22-23). They put a CRIMSON CLOAK and CROWN of thorns on His head. The CYRENE CARRIED his CROSS. At CHRIST'S death the CENTURION said, "He was the Son of God."

28. (R2) At His RESURRECTION, the ROCK was ROLLED away. The angel told Mary, "He is RISEN." She RAN to tell the disciples of His RESURRECTION and that He was RISEN. When the disciples saw Jesus, He said, "Go make disciples. REMEMBER, I am with you always" (Mt. 28:20).

Heaven Can Wait WWII Leather Bomber
Jacket Patch

During WWII there were at least eleven different B-17s named "Heaven Can Wait." The leather insignia above is an example of a flight jacket patch for the B-17 by that name from the 401st Bomb Group, the 612th Squadron of the 8th US Army Air Force. The name of the B-17 was taken from the 1943 movie comedy and song...*Heaven Can Wait.*

THE ABCs OF HEAVEN

Rejoice and be glad: for great is your reward in heaven (Matt. 5:12).

Numerous nationally recognized opinion polls indicate most Americans believe in heaven. The majority of the major religions of the world believe in heaven or an afterlife filled with joy and peace. The term "heaven" is used in the Bible more than 700 times. The only human requirement to enter heaven is death. The major religions of the world differ significantly in their opinion about the spiritual requirements to enter heaven.

A number of years ago I was visiting with a World War II veteran. He said, "Doc, you probably think I am really old and that I should be ready to die. But I'm not ready to die. I feel good and my mind is clear. It's not that I'm afraid to die. I'm not. I have a

Christian faith. In fact, I believe that when I die I'm going to go to heaven, but I just don't want to catch the first bus." I guess most of us feel that way...most of us don't want to catch the first bus.

In *A Gathering of Eagles*, VADM Art Cebrowski, USA, (Ret) offered this advice for life about goals:

> Young men and women are rightly encouraged to establish goals and work toward them with diligence, courage, and tenacity. But how is one to establish a goal? Many define their goals in terms such as, "achieve command of a combat unit, become president of a major corporation, achieve some considerable net worth, or attain high rank." The trouble with these goals is that on attaining them one is left with two awkward questions: Is that all there is? What's next? Rather, a goal should be lofty, laudable, and one which can be continually strived for but never fully attained even in a long life of dedication. And when someone says, "Well, that is fine, but what is your ultimate goal?" you will be able to respond, "Heaven."

Desmond Doss received the Medal of Honor in WWII as a combat medic with the 77th Infantry Division on Okinawa. Doss was a conscientious objector who would not even touch a weapon and refused to carry one. His company commander tried to have Doss kicked out of the Army. The Department of the Army allowed Doss to remain in the military even though he refused to carry a weapon. Doss did not feel that he could take a life but wanted to be allowed to serve, hoping to save lives. During the war, Doss saved the lives of hundreds of soldiers including the life of the company commander who tried to have him kicked out of the Army. The commander later said of Doss, "The man I tried to have kicked out of the Army as a coward is, in fact, the bravest man I have ever met."

Desmond Doss offered this advice for life in *VALOR*:

> I would like to share my godly mother's advice: Live by the Golden Rule, and do unto others as you would have them do unto you. Study the Bible daily for it is God's love letter to us

letting us know right from wrong; it is our roadmap to heaven. He has not asked us to give up anything good, only that which is not good enough for life eternal with Him and our loved ones. Eye hath not seen nor ear heard, neither hath it entered into the heart of man the wonderful things He has gone to prepare for us who love him and keep His holy law. If we miss heaven, we have missed everything.

I periodically say, "I don't have a tattoo, but if I was going to get one it would say: 'If we miss heaven, we have missed everything.'" I often wear a bracelet on my wrist with that quote by Desmond. Over the years, I have read many stories of individuals who have had a "near-death experience." The majority of these individuals describe heaven as a place of indescribable peace and joy. A very small percentage of individuals described something totally different. They described their near-death experience in hell and say that it was the most frightening and horrible experience of their lives.

Currently the book, *Heaven Is for Real*, remains on many bestselling book lists. It is about a young boy named Colton Burpo who had surgery for a ruptured appendix. He went to heaven, returned, and later explained the experience to his parents, describing who he met and what he saw in heaven.

Heaven is the eternal destination for those who have a Christian faith. In John 14:6 we read, "Jesus answered, 'I am the way, the truth, and the life. No one comes to the Father except through me.'" This faith allows all who are willing to acknowledge Christ as Lord and Savior the opportunity of eternal peace and joy in heaven. Some might ask, "If there really is a heaven, how can I go there? If Jesus is the only way to heaven, how can I know him?

The ABCs of The Sinner's Prayer
It's as easy as ABC:

A. "ADMIT that you are a sinner" (Romans 3:23).

B. BELIEVE. "Confess with your mouth that Jesus is Lord, and

141

BELIEVE in your heart that God raised him from the dead, and you shall be saved."(Romans 10:9).

C. CALL on. "Whosoever shall CALL on (CONFESS) the name of the Lord will be saved." (Romans 10:13).

If you have not already done so, I would like to encourage you to begin your relationship with Jesus Christ right now and begin your journey toward heaven.

Part 4

Songs and Oaths

Civil War Officer and Enlisted Soldier Kepi Hat Insignia

These are examples of a Civil War Infantry officer's brass bugle forage hat insignia with false embroidery pattern and a plain stamped brass bugle used by the enlisted soldier of the Union Infantry. The use of the bugle insignia led to the periodic descriptions by infantry soldiers as being part of "The boys in the band."

AMERICA THE BEAUTIFUL
First verse of seven:

O beautiful for spacious skies
For amber waves of grain,
For purple mountain majesties
Above the fruited plain!

America, America!
God shed His grace on thee
And crown thy good with brotherhood
From sea to shining sea!

GOD BLESS AMERICA

While the storm clouds gather far across the sea,
Let us swear allegiance to a land that's free.
Let us all be grateful for a land so fair,
As we raise our voices in a solemn prayer.
God bless America,
Land that I love.
Stand beside her, and guide her
Through the night with a light from above.
From the mountains, to the prairies,
To the oceans, white with foam,
God bless America,
My home, sweet home.

STAR SPANGLED BANNER

First verse of four:

Oh, say can you see, by the dawn's early light
What so proudly we hailed at the twilight's last gleaming?
Whose broad stripes and bright stars, thru the perilous fight,
O'er the ramparts we watched, were so gallantly streaming?
And the rockets' red glare, the bombs bursting in air,
Gave proof through the night that our flag was still there.
O say, does that star-spangled banner yet wave
O'er the land of the free and the home of the brave?

MY COUNTRY, 'TIS OF THEE
Also known as AMERICA

First and second verses:
My country, 'tis of thee,

Sweet land of liberty, Of thee I Sing;
Land where my fathers died,
Land of the pilgrims' pride,
From ev'ry mountainside
Let freedom ring!

My native country, thee,
Land of the noble free,
Thy name I love;
I love thy rocks and rills,
Thy woods and templed hills;
My heart with rapture thrills,
Like that above.

BATTLE HYMN OF THE REPUBLIC

First and second verses:

Mine eyes have seen the glory of the coming of the Lord;
He is tramping out the vintage where the grapes of wrath are
stored;
He hath loosed the fateful lightning of His terrible swift sword;
His truth is marching on.
(Chorus)
Glory, glory, hallelujah!
Glory, glory, hallelujah!
Glory, glory, hallelujah!
His truth is marching on.

I have seen Him in the watch-fires of a hundred circling camps,
They have builded Him an altar in the evening dews and damps;
I can read His righteous sentence by the dim and flaring lamps:
His day is marching on.

ONWARD CHRISTIAN SOLDIERS

First verse of four:

Onward, Christian soldiers!
Marching as to war,
With the cross of Jesus
Going on before.
Christ, the royal Master,
Leads against the foe;
Forward into battle,
See His banners go!
Onward Christian soldiers!
Marching as to war,
With the cross of Jesus,
Going on before.

WWII Paratrooper
48-star American Flag Sleeve Insignia

PLEDGE OF ALLEGIANCE

I pledge allegiance to the Flag of the United States of America, and to the Republic for which it stands, one Nation under God, indivisible, with liberty and justice for all.

The following story is from Senator John McCain and is included in *Prisoners of Hope*.

As you may know, I spent five and one-half years as a prisoner of war during the Vietnam War. In the early years of imprisonment, the North Vietnamese kept us in solitary confinement or with two or three to a cell. In 1971, the North Vietnamese moved us from these conditions of isolation into large rooms with as many as 30 to 40 men to a room. This was, as you can imagine, a wonderful change and was a direct result of the efforts of millions of Americans on behalf of a few hundred POWs 10,000 miles from home.

One of the men who moved into my room was a young man named Mike Christian. Mike came from a small town near Selma, Alabama. He hadn't worn a pair of shoes until he was 13 years old. At 17, he enlisted in the U.S. Navy. He later earned a commission by going to Officer Candidate School. He then became a Naval Flight Officer and was shot down and captured in 1967. Mike had a keen and deep appreciation of the opportunities this country and our military provide for people who want to work and want to succeed.

As part of the change in treatment, the Vietnamese allowed some prisoners to receive packages from home. In some of these packages were handkerchiefs, scarves, and other items of clothing. Mike got himself a bamboo needle. Over a period of a couple of months, he created an American flag and sewed it on the inside of his shirt. Every afternoon, before we had a bowl of soup, we would hang Mike's shirt on the wall of the cell and say the Pledge of Allegiance. I know the Pledge of Allegiance may not seem the most important part of our day now, but I can assure you that in that stark cell it was indeed the most important event.

One day the Vietnamese searched our cell, as they did periodically, and discovered Mike's shirt with the flag sewn inside and removed it. That evening they returned, opened the cell, and for the benefit of all, they beat Mike Christian severely for the next couple of hours. Then they opened the door of the cell once again and threw him back in. We cleaned him up as best we could.

The cell in which we lived had a concrete slab in the middle on which we slept. Four naked light bulbs hung in each corner of the room. As I said, we tried to clean up Mike as well as we could. After the excitement died down, I looked in the corner of the room, and sitting there beneath that dim light bulb was my friend, Mike Christian. He was sitting there with his eyes almost swollen shut from the beating he had received, making another American flag. He was not making that flag because it made Mike Christian feel better. He was making that flag because he knew how important it was to us to be able to pledge our allegiance to our flag and our country.

So, the next time you say the Pledge of Allegiance, you must never forget the sacrifice and courage that thousands of Americans have made to build our nation and promote freedom around the world. You must remember our duty, our honor, our country.

Clarence Larsen offered this statement in *Prisoners of Hope*, "Honor your flag. It spells freedom—yours and mine—and that freedom comes at a terrible price." Mr. Larsen was a Japanese POW for 3-1/2 years during WWII. He survived the Bataan Death March, the Hell Ship Nissyo Maru, and one year of slave labor in Japan.

Private First Class to Command Sergeant Major

UNIFORMED SERVICES OATH OF OFFICE (ENLISTED)

I (NAME), do solemnly swear that I will support and defend the Constitution of the United States against all enemies foreign and domestic; that I will bear true faith and allegiance to the same; and that I will obey the orders of the President of the United States and the orders of the officers appointed over me, according to the regulations and the Uniform Code of Military Justice. So help me God.

2nd Lieutenant to GENERAL

UNIFORMED SERVICES OATH OF OFFICE (OFFICER)

I, (NAME), do solemnly swear that I will support and defend the

Constitution of the United States against all enemies, foreign and domestic; that I will bear true faith and allegiance to the same; that I take this obligation freely, without any mental reservation or purpose of evasion; and that I will well and faithfully discharge the duties of the office on which I am about to enter. So help me God.

Part 5

Prisoners of HOPE

ADVICE FOR LIFE and STORIES
from men who ring the cover of the book
PRISONERS OF HOPE—A GATHERING OF EAGLES

Colonel Fred Cherry
U.S. Air Force (Ret.) • Vietnam

My seven and a half years as a POW in North Vietnam will always have an impact on my life. I survived the pain, torture, isolation, loneliness, and hopelessness through my faith in God, family, country, fellow prisoners, and self. I relied on my Christian faith to get me through the toughest times. I was thankful for my Christian upbringing and the values which I had been taught by my family, elders, and teachers. When all hope seemed to fade and creep away, my faith would grasp the fading hope and reel it back within my reach. Without the sound values deeply imbedded in me, my performance as an American fighting man in the hands of the enemy would have been miserable and so would my ability to face myself in a mirror today.

We must continue to teach our young people the sound values which have been the foundation for all great people and nations. Our youth are our future, and the survival of our nation will depend on leadership. We must develop leaders with unwavering integrity, honesty, moral character, and love. Young Americans: Have faith, set your goals high, and aspire to be the best that you can be. Build your foundation on the values that have made great men, women, and nations.

HONOR, INTEGRITY, FAITH IN GOD

I am an authentic American citizen of Native American and African heritage. I grew up in a rural area of Virginia, near Suffolk, the youngest of eight children. There were four boys and four girls. We were a very close family. It seemed as though everyone in the neighborhood were members of one big family. The neighbors felt responsible to help rear and raise everyone else's kids. My family was a religious family so we were in the Baptist church every Sunday. All during my youth I was taught what was right and what was wrong, and I was expected to always do what was right.

I was very young when I first had a desire to fly. During WWII, my home was near a Navy auxiliary base that was used to practice carrier landings on a regular runway. As a young boy, I would often watch these planes, and my desire to become a pilot grew. About the same time, the Tuskegee Airmen shipped to Italy and North Africa. The story of these heroes only increased my desire to fly, although my family always thought and maybe hoped I would become a doctor.

After high school I went to college and I took all the tests to see if I could join the Air Force and become a pilot. I was accepted, then enlisted in the Air Force, awaited assignment to flight training, completed my training, and was commissioned a second lieutenant. In a short period of time, I began flying combat missions in Korea and flew over 50 combat sorties during the Korean War.

After the Korean War, I remained in the Air Force, and seven years later, I was assigned to Japan for five years. In 1965 I flew combat missions over North Vietnam. I was flying a F-105 Thunder Chief out of Thailand when I was shot down in October 1965. When my aircraft was hit by anti-aircraft fire, the cockpit began to fill with smoke. The plane exploded and I ejected at about 400 feet at over 600 miles an hour. In the process of ejection, I broke my left ankle, my left wrist, and crushed my left shoulder. I was captured immediately upon landing by Vietnamese militia and civilians. Thus began my seven and a half years as a prisoner of war. I experienced some very brutal treatment. I spent 702 days in solitary confinement, the longest period of time was for 53 weeks. At one time I was either tortured or in punishment for 93 straight days.

During my life I have certainly experienced some memorable times. I believe good conquers evil, and that there is no substitute for honor, integrity, love, and faith. I am convinced that faith in God, country, our fellow man, and one's self will help to overcome any situation during the toughest of times.

I know that the faith in God, and love and respect for my fellow man that my parents and family instilled in me during my youth carried me through some very difficult years as a POW in Vietnam. I was always taught to love and respect others and forgive those who mistreat, scorn, or persecute me. Righteousness will prevail, and evil will be overcome.

That same love, honor, integrity, respect, faith, and will to forgive have always guided me in every endeavor and walk of life. They have allowed me to overcome the damages of discrimination, Jim Crow, and the social and economic barriers associated with growing up a poor dirt farmer.

We have choices to make in life. We need to be concerned that we make the right choices. I strongly advocate that every choice we make be based upon some standard. My standard for making decisions is based on doing what is right, or what some might call, "doing the right thing." I use as my embedded standard: honor, integrity, faith in God and country, and love. Believe that right will prevail over wrong. Know that honor, integrity, faith in God and country, respect, and love will set you free.

Rear Admiral Jeremiah Denton
U.S. Navy (Ret.) • Vietnam

My creed for life is the Apostles' Creed. My code of conduct is derived from the Ten Commandments and Jesus' command to "love God, and love your neighbor as you love yourself." As an American naval officer, I derived motivation to serve my nation because of my love for my country. I also believe that Americans have a special justification to love their country derived from a love of God. America was founded as "one nation under God." Our founding fathers deliberately based their experiment in democracy upon the premise that the compassion and the self-discipline required for the success of a democracy can only come from citizens who believe strongly in God.

Due to our nation's founding premise, I found it easy to serve in a profession that protected our land. My generation helped to protect and ensure the survival of our nation against Fascism and Soviet Communism. Now our greatest enemy is the threat that would do away with America's belief in the founding premise, its founding thesis.

If we continue to increase our forgetfulness of God's ultimate significance, then America will not survive. I strive for the ultimate significant success—heaven—by loving and serving God, country, and family.

THE SACRED HEART OF JESUS

To those who are non-Catholics among the readers, let me preface my story with an explanation of the Roman Catholic devotion to "The Sacred Heart of Jesus." Jesus, of course, has both a human and divine nature and took on a human body, and all the natural characteristics of a human when He was on earth. His brain and sensory system enabled Him to think and feel as a human being. His divine nature rendered Him a sinless soul but He felt the temptations of a human being, and all the physical pains, pleasures, sights, and emotions of a human being. Thus the immensity of His suffering for our salvation is more palpably understood and appreciated by us. It is a Catholic tradition to regard His heart as the center, the symbol of His own humanity, the "source" of His human compassion and His love as He felt it and showed it on earth.

The love resulting in the miracle of Cana is one example of what could be attributed to His Sacred Heart. We feel we can "get to Him" better, if you will, by appealing to that copiously loving heart. I had adopted that devotion and frequently uttered the prayer, "Sacred Heart of Jesus, I place my trust in Thee," which was the standard prayer of that devotion. I said it frequently, at least every night in prison.

Okay, with that said, let's go back to 1967, about two years after I was shot down. Those years were probably the worst in terms of suffering for me. For a considerable portion of that time I had served as senior officer for all the American POWs, responsible for issuing orders defining specific lines of resistance on unexpected challenges which arose, representing complaints about our treatment to our captors, and generally feeling responsible for our morale and performance of duty. Simply being a POW involved plenty of stress, along with long periods of physical and mental suffering. But for those finding themselves senior over an isolated group of POWs, there was extra pressure.

The context of the timeframe of the incident I am about to relate was in the middle of the four years of intense mistreatment: mid 1967. Robbie Risner, then I, then Jim Stockdale had served as Senior Ranking Officer, (SRO), in that sequence since October 1965 when the torture began. At this particular point in time, they were both isolated, and I was trying to act as SRO again in a camp called "Las Vegas" where most of the POWs were being kept. Vegas was like a hotel with fairly small cells, most of them were sharing common walls with one or two other cells.

Many of us had been moved to Vegas from the "Zoo" where there were separate buildings, perhaps eight, holding a total of upwards of 100 prisoners. This arrangement permitted the North Vietnamese to erect bamboo walls cutting off visual contact between the buildings, which greatly impeded our audio contact because the walls limited maximum range of sound. The guards could use the walls to hide behind and catch people in one building trying to communicate with one another. Torture was always bestowed on POWs caught communicating, along with other unpleasant measures intended to intimidate the men from communicating in the future. This rendered communications difficult compared to the Vegas situation. We had been doing pretty well with tapping on the walls at Vegas for a number of months, but then the purge came that caused Stockdale's temporary isolation, and I inherited the sack.

To inhibit and virtually prevent me from communicating as SRO, they stationed a guard in a chair at the door of my cell. At all times, his chair was leaned back against the door, and the back of his head rested against the door. The acoustics were such that he could easily hear any tap, no matter how soft. Communications and prayer were by far the biggest factors supporting our morale and performance of duty.

At that time morale was low for three reasons: First, for a number of months, torture was being applied more intensely because the war was being intensified. The enemy was in an ugly mood, and we knew prisoners were being promptly and severely tortured. We could hear their screams from a distance in another part of the prison complex. A purge among those POWs who had been in captivity longer was underway in an effort to break our chain of command and destroy our will to resist. Second, the news about the war which we were receiving made it evident that it was extremely unlikely the POWs would be released in any reasonable or early timeframe, and the conclusions that we would never be released were floating around in our minds. Third, communication was almost nil.

I was intensely frustrated and chagrined at my lack of ability to communicate. Though I would have never admitted it, I was also of the belief that the U.S. was beginning to experience a growing anti-war movement. This sentiment would not likely improve our victory chances or any escalation of the scope and intensity of the U.S. offensive campaign, which many of us felt was necessary. Less importantly but of considerable effect on us, the end of the war did indeed seem further away, and release less certain. The screams of the prisoners in torture did not help my morale.

During this phase I was enjoying the company of Jim Mulligan, my occasional cellmate. At this point in time, Jim was sleeping in the upper bunk. It was midday, siesta time, and the screams occasionally broke the normal silence for that time of day. I was praying, as usual, that God's will be done, but that I hoped His will would include, among other things, improving our present situation because I was in leg irons and a guard was looking right at me. I prayed especially that He would let me come up with a means of communications that could be effectively used even when I was unable to move. Finally, as my last prayer, with special earnestness, I uttered the words, "Sacred Heart of Jesus, I place my trust in Thee."

In only a few seconds, I clearly heard an incredibly kind, dignified, but commanding voice, which I took to be the voice of Jesus Himself. The voice said clearly and rather slowly, "Say, Sacred Heart of Jesus, I give myself to You." I was almost knocked down with a wave of awe upon hearing the voice. It was the most real and the most amazing thing that ever happened to me. The speaker of those words, of course, was not only assuring me of having heard my prayer, but had instructed me to deliver it in the future with new wording and meaning. I was not to say I merely trusted Him, but transcending that, I was to GIVE MYSELF (all of me, all of my concerns) not just to THEE, as to a formal, omnipotent other type of supreme being, but to give myself to YOU, the familiar designation of a friend or a brother. And the tone and inflection of the voice conveyed the same mood of brotherly familiarity and assurance.

It may sound kooky, but I know it happened, and I know it was real, more than I know my name is what it is, or that my wife is really my wife. For what it is worth, I can assure you that for me the prayer has worked. A few months later at a camp called Alcatraz where eleven of us were isolated for over two years, I did have a brainstorm which permitted me to devise the reliable, undetectable communications method for which I had specifically prayed. In many other painful situations, the prayer has since brought relief to me and to others who used it after I confided to them about the prayer.

Commander Porter Halyburton
U.S. Navy (Ret.) • Vietnam

All through the seven and a half years of imprisonment in North Vietnam, my Christian faith was a constant source of great strength and comfort. I knew that this was something that my captors could never take away from me. Had they been able to destroy that faith, I do not think that I would have survived with any sense of integrity or honor. The struggle to live an honorable life and to find meaning in that life, no matter how miserable the circumstances, was the most important thing I could do.

Over time I developed what I refer to as a Life Statement. It is as follows: I wish, at the instant of my death, to be able to look back upon a full and fruitful Christian life, lived as an honest man who has constantly striven to improve himself and the world in which he lives, and to die forgiven by God, and have, with a clear conscience, the love and respect of my family and friends, and the peace of the Lord in my soul.

A WORSE PLACE

Two days after being shot down northwest of Hanoi in October 1965, I arrived at the Hoa Lo prison, the now-famous Hanoi

160

Hilton. I was put in a small cell in an area that Americans called Heartbreak Hotel, and I was to find that this was a most appropriate name. Interrogations began immediately and increased in frequency and intensity. Every time I answered with "Name, Rank, Service Number and Date of Birth"—the only information permitted by the Code of Conduct.

After two weeks of threats, beatings, humiliations, and filthy conditions, the Rabbit (one of our guards) finally gave me an ultimatum in the form of a choice—to answer questions and move to a "nice camp" where I could be with my friends and enjoy good treatment and food, or to continue to refuse to cooperate and be moved to a much worse place where I would be alone and be punished for my bad attitude. Heartbreak was pretty grim—tiny cells with concrete bunks and built-in leg irons, so I could hardly imagine anything worse.

Actually the choice was pretty easy at this point. My prayers and the advice from other Americans in Heartbreak gave me strength and some confidence. There was nothing I couldn't live with. I did not believe there was a better place, and I was not going to give them anything in any case. So I chose the worse one. Sure enough, it was worse, but different. It was a larger cell in a building that had been named "The Office" in a prison called the "Zoo." The exterior was pleasant enough—it had been a film studio used by the propaganda branch of the army with stucco building and red tile roofs, a swimming pool in the center, and various kinds of trees. On the inside, the windows had all been barred and then bricked up on the inside to within three inches of the top. Since I had been moved in the middle of the night, the cell was completely dark and I had to feel my way around the walls to even know how big it was. The floor was covered in dust and smelled of wet concrete. This smell and the bleakness and the blackness of the cell got to me that night, and I felt some of the terror that Fortunato, Poe's character in the "The Cask of Amontillado," must have felt as he realized that he had been bricked up in the cellar. I longed for and prayed for something green, something alive, and something friendly.

One morning very early I heard a faint scraping at the window, almost an invitation to investigate. I jumped and grabbed the top bricks in the window and struggled up far enough to look over. And there, sticking through the slats of the shutter but beyond the bars, was a green leaf. It was the most beautiful leaf that I had ever seen, and I knew at once that God had instructed the tree outside to move its branch just enough to present me with this gift, this sign that I was not alone. The cell, as well as my spirits, brightened up considerably.

I also received another gift while I was there—a little extra food and a bit of humor. The turnkey appeared unexpectedly one day and gave me two pieces of paper and a small dish containing a little ball of rice. The papers contained the Camp Regulations, one in English and the other in Vietnamese. He pointed to the wall and then left. I thought, This is pretty cool—something to read and a little snack. When the guard returned, he was furious that I had eaten the "glue" and had not pasted the regulations on the wall as I was supposed to. He must have thought that I was the dumbest person on earth, and he dutifully showed me how to use the rice to stick the papers to the wall. At this point I decided that playing dumb was probably a good thing to do and would probably work.

Interrogations continued day after day. "Where you from? What kind of aircraft you fly? How many missions you fly?" And again, the same old threat—cooperate or you will move to a much worse place. Soon enough the threat became a reality, and I was awakened in the middle of the night and blindfolded. With my meager bedroll under one arm, I was led across the prison to the back side of a large building that I knew was called the "Auditorium."

My new home was a storage room in the back, up a few steps from the central room that had been used for larger groups to view films. It had no light but the window had not been bricked up, although it did have bars and tight-fitting shutters. Again I had to feel my way around the cell in the dark and found that it was quite small. I tapped on the wall opposite the window but got no response. I realized that I was not only alone but isolated from the other prisoners. Before finally going to sleep on the cold cement floor, I prayed to God for a long time and asked for strength to endure what was to come. It was the uncertainty of what lay in the future that was so hard to deal with. However, I had my leaf, and I had faith that God was not going to abandon me in this place.

In the morning, as the wake-up gong was sounded, I woke to a dim light to see just how small and miserable my confinement was. From the Vietnamese voices outside the window, I realized that I was close to the "Head Shed" which contained the interrogation rooms and administrative offices. How could I endure such proximity to my tormentors?

About mid-morning, the gloom was pierced by a beam of sunlight shining through an undiscovered crack in the shutters. It struck the opposite wall with a sharp brilliance—surely a sign from God once again. Quickly I made a small paper cross from the scrap of what served as toilet paper and glued it to the wall with some rice grains just at the spot where the sun had struck. Each day, as the sunlight illuminated the little cross, I felt the presence of God and it sustained me throughout that lonely and difficult time.

Once again came the demand for a choice—cooperate or go to a worse place. All the way across the prison next to the back wall was a small shed that had been used to store coal, among other things. It was infested with ants, mosquitoes, geckos, and, at night, rats. I was finally convinced that this was really the worst place they had. Food that was barely edible to begin with was left outside the door for hours, and when I got it, it was covered with ants. I was weak from constant diarrhea, sleepless nights, and constant interrogation, humiliation, beatings, and loneliness throughout each day. After several weeks, I was very close to the end of my strength and resolve. The worst part was having no one to talk to, so my prayers were for strength and companionship. When the time came again to choose, I was not sure I could survive for long in a place worse than this shed, and I was tempted to try and get them off my back by answering a few questions. Luckily, I did not give in because their idea of the worst place was putting me in a cell with a black man. I was ordered to care for him as he was badly injured and could do nothing for himself. The Vietnamese must have thought that forcing us together in this situation would set us against each other and break us down.

Major Fred Cherry and I lived together for eight months, and the Vietnamese plan did not work. Fred nearly died several times during that time, but he was too determined and much too tough to die. He says that I saved his life, but he is the one who probably saved mine. He was indeed a gift from God and the answer to my prayers. We became lifelong friends, and it was his example of courage, patriotism, devotion to duty, and personal integrity that set a high standard during those difficult years that followed. The night we were moved apart was one of the saddest of my life, and we were both to go back into solitary confinement and endure serious torture to force our cooperation. It was strength from God and what I learned from Fred that helped me get through that terrible time.

Colonel Roger Ingvalson
U.S. Air Force (Ret.) • Vietnam

All success is secular; all significance is spiritual. My goals in life changed after I was shot down and captured by the North Vietnamese just prior to my 40th birthday. It was on this day that Jesus Christ performed a miracle by sparing my life after ejection from my jet fighter at an extremely high speed. That day I became a Christian. My first 18 years of active duty in the US Air Force were spent attempting to achieve success in the secular world. Then, through my relationship with Christ, I realized that success was meaningless without having significance in life. Leadership by example became my motto as a military leader. My walk must equal my talk. I never gave an order without insuring that I could do it myself. After 26 years, I retired from the Air Force and formed a prison ministry. During the 15 years that I ministered to inmates, it was evident to me that unless I demonstrated a significance in my life, it was futile to expect to see a change in inmates' lives.

MIRACLE

It was May 28, 1968. The air war in Vietnam had been going on for three and a half years. My mission was to lead a flight to destroy a bridge in North Vietnam. We both had an air to ground missile hung under each wing. It was a good assignment—literally no defenses, or so I thought. We were successful in destroying the target. This was my 87th mission, and with 1600 hours in the F-105, I was confident that I could hit any target. As we pulled off the target, an Air Controller requested that we hit an enemy convoy of trucks. Having a full load of 20 mm available, I jumped at the chance to destroy the trucks. My philosophy was that it was a waste of mission to engage a ground target unless I destroyed it. I believed in high speed and low altitude engagement in order to assure accuracy.

Locating the trucks, I rolled in doing approximately 500 knots, waiting until I was below 50 feet before I pulled the trigger and fired a long burst on the trucks. Then it happened—there were air defenses in the area. I heard and felt the explosion! My cockpit immediately filled with smoke. I hit the afterburner to gain valuable altitude, then pulled the canopy ejection handle to get rid of the smoke. I rocketed up to about 600 feet when my aircraft went into an uncontrollable roll. The problem was not only that I was no longer gaining altitude, but I was rapidly heading down. The situation was desperate. Ignoring ejection procedures and more by reflex, I pulled the ejection seat handle and squeezed the trigger. That's the last thing I remembered until I regained consciousness just before hitting the ground. I realized that I was doomed for capture. My freedom was about to be lost to dozens of people racing toward me, yelling in an angry foreign tongue.

As I hit the ground, my first thought and reaction was to feel for broken bones. With 15 years of fighter aircraft experience, I was fully aware of the fact that there is very little chance of survival during an emergency ejection, at high speed and low altitude, without a multitude of injuries and fractured bones. To my amazement, I had no broken bones or other injuries.

I had spent my entire 40 years of life regularly attending church, but I was not a Christian. With my knowledge of the Bible,

I knew that Jesus Christ performed miracles, and there was no doubt in my mind that this was a miracle. The Lord got my attention, so in the middle of this dried-up rice paddy with dozens of angry people getting ready to capture me, I prayed that Jesus Christ would take over my life.

I was captured immediately, but because of making the most important decision of my life, I survived almost five years of torture, starvation, and loneliness as a POW. Yes, it was the worst day of my life. I lost my freedom. However, it was also the best day of my life, because I gained new hope and the promise of eternal freedom in heaven!

Colonel Sam Johnson
U.S. Air Force (Ret.) • Vietnam

I spent 29 years in the Air Force and was proud to answer my nation's call to service in Korea and in Vietnam. The Air Force taught me the value of duty, honor, and country. And by its nature, the military is committed to excellence and success. We send young men to battle to fight for our freedom and for democracy to win. We should all strive for success, but what is it that makes us significant?

During my captivity I realized that my significance comes from God. I am nothing without Him, and while my military training prepared me well for my years of captivity, it was God who allowed my survival.

HIS MERCIES ARE NEW EVERY MORNING

As a Prisoner of War for nearly seven years, I went through some difficult times. I spent 42 months in solitary confinement and 74 days in stocks. I told about my days as a POW in my book, Captive Warrior: A Vietnam POW's Story.

On the evening of my 74th day in stocks, I stared at the boarded-up window of my cell. It had been so long since I had seen the sky and the sun. My eyes blurred with tears, and at that moment, I felt suddenly finished. It was over; I couldn't fight any more. I remember thinking as I fell asleep, exhausted and defeated, that it would be okay if I never woke up again.

Late that night a typhoon tore through the city of Hanoi, ripping roofs off buildings and lashing the prison courtyard with wind and slicing rain. I awoke to the sounds of breaking glass and slamming window shutters. The floor of my cell was filled with water, and I huddled against the wall, as far away from the incoming rain as the leg stocks would allow me. The violence of the storm stirred something inside me, and I began to pray like I had never prayed before. Long after the storm subsided, I lay on my bunk, drenched from the rain, and strangely at peace in the darkness.

I awoke the next morning to see my cell flooded with the first bright streaks of dawn. The storm had ripped the boards off my window, and for the first time in more than two months, sparkling rays of light danced a celebration in my tiny room. I had an overwhelming sense of the presence of God in that moment. He was with me, and He would be faithful. His fresh supply of mercy was pouring into my cell with all the reality of the sun's shining rays. I understood the Bible verse I learned as a child: "His mercies are new every morning." I was convinced that He would be sufficient for me; He would see me through.

Captain Eugene "Red" McDaniel
U.S. Navy (Ret.) • Vietnam

Success becomes significance when it fits into God's plan, when our accomplishments somehow further His kingdom here on earth. Often that kind of significant success is not seen as success when measured in human standards.

All my life I have strived to be successful: to be a great athlete in high school and college, to get "outstanding" on my naval officer fitness reports, to be a "top gun" naval aviator, to be a tough resister in a Communist prison, to be commanding officer of an aircraft carrier, to rise to the top in military rank, to found a defense policy organization that would have an impact, and to establish a thriving small business in my retirement. When measured by human standards, I've succeeded in those areas—and I have been duly rewarded by athletic scholarships, early selection for service rank, military awards and decorations for my performance as a POW, choice duty assignments, and the praise of men.

However, those rewards have not been my greatest rewards. My experience as a POW in Vietnam helped me to see the difference between success as measured by men and success as seen in the eyes of God. There were many times in my lonely cell when my victories were known only by me and God, and I found that those victories were profoundly more rewarding than the times I received a pat on the back or a military award. Since my return to freedom, the opportunities I've had to share with others the love of God that sustained me during my captivity have been infinitely more precious than my chestful of military decorations. Writing my book, *Scars and Stripes*, as a testament to God's faithfulness during those dark days has brought satisfaction not paralleled by anything else.

And by far, the greatest rewards have come from times when I've done something simply because it was the right thing to do, when I've been criticized, or even ostracized, for taking an unpopular stand on causes which look like failures in the eyes of the world. Then, just as in my lonely cell, God knows and I know, and that is enough. My success has become significance.

THE FINAL SERMON

The last sermon I had prepared as prison chaplain in Hanoi was constructed out of the gloom and despair I felt about never being released. Strangely, God took me to the Book of Job, to the story of a man who had his share of trials and yet recovered. I never did deliver it in Hanoi because we were released just before the Sunday service. Instead, we held that service at Clark Air Force Base in the Philippines after we landed.

The words I prepared under the inspiration of God's Spirit while in captivity, took on new meaning and perhaps even more pertinence when I spoke them in freedom. This is the part of the sermon that stands out for me even now; I still think of it whenever I am tempted to ask the reason for what I endured. Job was a righteous and upright man who had great wealth, more than any other man in the land. He had seven sons and three daughters. He was a holy man who loved God, and God loved him. But Satan was able to come between the Lord and Job, so Job lost all his wealth, little by little. His house was blown down. He lost his seven sons and his three daughters. He was covered with boils, and all the people turned their backs on Job. This went on for a significant period of time.

But Job fell down on his knees and worshiped God and never once lost his integrity. He did not renounce his faith in God, but endured all that Satan could offer. God held him in highest esteem and returned to him what he had lost. God said, "My son, remember well these words I have spoken to you. As long as you live, you will be subject to change, whether you like it or not: now glad, now sorrowing; now vigorous, now lazy; now gloomy, now merry. Without battle, no man can come to victory; the greater the battle, the greater the victory."

Colonel Norman McDaniel
U.S. Air Force (Ret.) • Vietnam

Who am I? Why am I here? How should I live? Correct answers to these questions and a personal, positive response to them is the key to a successful and significant life.

First, I realize that I am a creation of the One, True, Almighty, and Everlasting God: the God of the Universe, and the Father of my Lord and Savior, Jesus Christ. I realize that through Christ, I have a personal, living relationship with God that is everlasting.

Second, I realize that my purpose in this mortal life is to establish and strengthen a personal relationship with God and to fulfill the unique purpose for which He created me.

Third, I should live by nurturing a right relationship with God by being a minister of His (in helping the poor, needy, sick, suffering, and those who do not know Him or have not accepted Him) and by doing all that I do to His glory. Also, I should live by giving my devotion and energy (in the following priority) to God, family, country, others, and self while sincerely trusting in the Holy Spirit to maintain the right balance and the right emphasis at the right time.

I accepted Jesus Christ as my Lord and Savior 15 years before I was shot down over North Vietnam and captured in 1966 during the Vietnam War. I spent almost seven years as a POW. During those long, endless years of torture, deprivation, and uncertainty, I was no stranger to God. I prayed, trusted in Him, drew closer to Him during those trying, perilous times, and He sustained me.

My sincere advice to every person is found in the Bible, in Proverbs 3:5-6 which says, "Trust in the Lord with all thine heart; and lean not unto thine own understanding. In all thy ways acknowledge Him, and He shall direct thy paths."

I am persuaded that becoming aware of one's sinful condition, accepting Jesus Christ as your personal Savior, and then trusting in the Lord each day is the key to real and lasting significance!

KEEPING FAITH

The key to a meaningful life is knowing who you are, how you fit in the universe, and how to successfully meet the challenges of life. Those who are aware of this key and use it effectively are truly blessed. I learned early in life to operationalize Matthew 6:33, "Seek ye first the kingdom of God." Part of the operationalization is to be a man or woman of your word.

As an American POW in North Vietnam during the Vietnam War, I was tested many times on keeping faith in my country. During the winter of 1967, after being a POW for more than one and a half years, that faith was severely tested.

I was taken from my cell to an interrogation room. This interrogation was different from most of the previous ones. Usually it consisted of questions, threats, and torture, but never before with the NVN POW Camp Commander. On this day, sitting beside the Camp Commander were his Chief Propaganda Officer and another lesser ranking military officer. The initial part of the interrogation was extremely friendly with the Camp Commander asking (through an interpreter) about my health and treatment. He proceeded to explain that the war was very tough for everyone with many people on both sides dying and being killed, it could last for many years and become much worse for me, and that I might never see my family again. When asked what I thought of his statement, I just acknowledged that I might never see my family again. Then he made an offer. He said, "But as for you, if you will help us, we will help you. We can arrange for you to leave this prison camp and live in a neutral country, and your family can join you there. In that way, you can stay alive and be with your family again. All you have to do is write some letters, make some tapes, and make some appearances to help us win this war."

From a personal, selfish perspective, the offer was tempting. I could stay alive, I would not be tortured or worried about whether I'd live through the next moment, and I would be with my family again. However, from a professional, military warrior's perspective, the offer was a non-starter. In taking the oath as an Officer of the United States Air Force, I had sworn to support and defend the Constitution of the United States against all enemies, foreign and domestic, and that I would bear true faith and allegiance to the same. I was also committed to the U.S. Fighting Man's Code (Code of Conduct) that states in Article III, "I will accept neither parole nor special favors from the enemy."

The way the Vietnam War was going in 1967 with no end in sight, not accepting the Camp Commander's offer could have resulted in my dying (or being killed) while a prisoner and never seeing my family again. However, some things are worth dying for. For me, as an American POW in NVN, one of the things worth dying for was keeping faith with my country and fellow prisoners. This meant not collaborating with, aiding, or abetting the enemy to the extent that it would cause grave harm or death of my fellow prisoners, or cause me to return to my country feeling like, or being viewed as, a traitor. My answer to the Prison Camp Commander was, "I cannot accept your offer."

Some key guidance for a meaningful life is found in Psalms 15:4, "He that sweareth to his own hurt, and changeth not." This verse highlights the importance of being a man or woman of your word. That statement bears directly on integrity, loyalty, trust, and character.

As a POW I had an oath to keep, a Code of Conduct to follow, and a God to whom I must ultimately give an account for my life. Today, the last part of the previous sentence is still operative. If you haven't done so, I highly recommend that you also make it an operational part of your life.

Captain James Mulligan
U.S. Navy (Ret.) • Vietnam

I learned the importance of all human companionship while kept in solitary confinement for more than three and one half years. I could remember nothing bad about anyone I had ever known and would have given anything to have just one of them with me.

In my life the word commitment is the operative word for all those things I believe in: marriage, family, God, country, etc. You make a commitment to what you believe in, and you stand by that commitment.

The word "persistence" is my guideline to reach goals and objectives. Be persistent and never, ever give up, and eventually you will achieve what you are seeking. Remember that with God all things are possible! So learn to pray!

I was a POW for seven years in North Vietnam. During that period, I spent more than 42 months in solitary confinement, in a closet with three walls and a door. This experience left me with time to think about who I was and what I really believed in. I asked myself many questions, among them, "What are my real religious beliefs? What is my civic responsibility in American society?" I also asked, "What is important in becoming a good American? What should every American child learn in order to become a good citizen, and where should they obtain this information?"

After much reflection, I concluded that the United States is the product of western civilization and Judeo-Christian traditions, molded by the Age of Enlightenment. At that point I decided that if we were going to teach our children to be good Americans, we would have to do the following:

1. Our children need to read, study, understand, and live by the Ten Commandments.

2. Our children also need to read, study, understand, and live by the principles taught in the message from the Sermon on the Mount.

3. Our children need to read, study, understand, and live by the Constitution of the United States and the Bill of Rights.

The rules of behavior set for us in these documents are the foundation of our democratic republic. Collectively, they signify what American citizens are all about. If all of us follow what they prescribe, we will never confuse true freedom with crass permissiveness.

Further, I believe that these concepts apply equally to Americans of all religions, races, colors, and nationalities. These concepts, these tenets, are the glue that holds all of us together in this great American experiment. They are what make us one nation under God, allowing us to experience liberty and justice for all.

Our children must understand that the freedoms we enjoy as American citizens were never freely given but were obtained with blood, sweat, tears, pain, and loss of life. They have to understand that for every right and every privilege they enjoy, they have a corresponding obligation and duty.

Every generation of Americans must understand that our democratic republic with its representative government is a fragile system. It must be nurtured and the founding principles have to be respected. Without any of these we are doomed to return to either tyranny or anarchical slavery, and the noble experiment will have failed. The choice falls upon every American. There is a burden to carry and every citizen must share it equally.

Brigadier General Robinson Risner
U.S. Air Force (Ret.) • Vietnam

Few people have reached their goals without determination. During my 33-year Air Force career, I was surrounded by people who were better educated, had a higher IQ, and many with greater talent. However, few had more determination. In addition, I had a strong faith in God. Determination and faith in God are the lynch pins that will take you to your goal.

YOU PASSED

When I was a child, my older brother learned how to fly small airplanes and that became my dream. World War II started when I was in high school, and I dreamed of becoming a fighter pilot. During high school I decided to attend Bible College, but I still wanted to be a pilot. I was only 17 when I graduated from high school and really wanted to enter the Aviation Cadet Program. One of the requirements to be accepted into the program was that you had to be a college graduate. I realized that I didn't have a chance, but one day while reading the paper, I read an article that said if you could pass a two-year college entrance exam, then you could apply to become an aviation cadet. I was only a mediocre student, but I immediately began to pray about the opportunity. Previously I had decided that I was going to go to Bible College, but I prayed, "Lord, if it is okay for me to go into the military...help me pass that test."

I was accepted to take the four hour examination. I was the last one to complete it. Everyone else had already finished and left. I handed my test to the sergeant who administered the test and started to leave. He said, "Wait a minute. We're not supposed to give out scores, but in your case, I'm going to make an exception." He graded the test, looked up at me, and said, "You passed by one point." I knew the Lord was saying, "It's OK."

In Vietnam I came to the conclusion that nothing was more important than a faith in God. Before imprisonment many of us had been too busy to put God first in our lives. A North Vietnamese prison cell changed that. We learned to feel at ease in talking about God, and we shared our doubts and faith. We prayed for one another and spent time praying together for all kinds of things. Our faith in God was essential. Without it, I could not have survived.

Note: the following are also taken
from the book, *Prisoners of Hope*.

Colonel William Byrns
U.S. Air Force (Ret.) • Vietnam

The military trains us mentally and physically to be leaders. It truly is the best training in the world. The key to successful leadership is the development of the spiritual part of our being. I have noticed, over my 30 years of service, that the most outstanding leaders I have met have a deep faith in God. Some of those leaders have had to lead under extremely adverse conditions such as in combat and in a prisoner of war situation. The North Vietnamese were able to eventually weaken us mentally and physically but could not weaken us spiritually. Without Jesus Christ as my Lord and Savior, I could not have made it. The core values of integrity, service, and excellence are critical to leadership and can be absolute when we are mentally, physically, and spiritually developed as leaders. The combination then produces character. Character is doing the right thing when no one else, except God, is looking.

THE TASTE OF FREEDOM
It was the afternoon of May 23, 1972, at Ubon Air Base, Thailand. My weapon systems Operator, Captain Ray Bean and I briefed the combat mission and proceeded to our F-4D Phantom.

On the way I met a high school classmate of mine who had landed with battle damage. I had not seen Doug Holmes for many years. It is a small world considering we only had 67 members in our class. After visiting briefly, goodbyes were said and I pressed on with the intended mission, not knowing I would not see Doug again for a year and a half.

There were no problems with the flight up until the shoot-down. We were on a five hour flight with numerous air-to-air refuelings. The mission was scheduled as a FAC (Forward Air Controller) mission into North Vietnam. Our job was to find targets (trucks, tanks, artillery, etc.) and direct fire on them from airborne fighters. We were able to locate enemy trucks and tanks moving toward South Vietnam. Our area of operation was Route Pack I, about 15 miles north of the Demilitarized Zone and about ten miles inland from the coast. SAMs (Surface to Air Missiles) were fired at us as well as the flight of F-4s we were working with in the target area. We had to jink (maneuver) numerous times to avoid being hit, but finally we were hit by 57-MM anti-aircraft fire. Our aircraft caught fire and began spinning out of control. After making a Mayday call, I said we were getting out of the aircraft, and I ejected both of us.

It was already dusk and hard for the enemy to see our parachutes; however, they still shot at us as we descended to earth. I would not see Ray again for three days. When I hit the ground, I went through all the survival procedures that I had been taught. The next step after landing was to hide my parachute and find a good place to hide myself. At this time I made a call on my survival radio to let the friendly fighters overhead know that I was down and okay. The terrain was rough with bomb craters and small hills. The only real cover was thick brush about six to ten feet high. I found a good place to hide in a huge bush with a hollowed out area and I dug in.

After getting settled in my hiding place, I again contacted the fighter overhead, and they were able to determine my exact position. I could hear enemy soldiers searching for us and saw them shooting in the bushes at other positions. They were trying to frighten me, and it was working fairly well. I pulled out the 38-caliber revolver that each of us carried. The first chamber of the cylinder of the revolver was kept empty for safety reasons. The squadron commander ordered that the first bullet be removed because of an accident in the squadron when a pilot accidentally shot himself in the thigh. As I pulled the pistol from the holster, I quickly realized a gun fight with a multitude of enemy soldiers was futile. I holstered the weapon and then proceeded to try to make contact again with the rescue forces and was told that they were trying to get helicopters into the area for our rescue.

As it grew darker and night settled in, word came that there was too much anti-aircraft fire and SAMs to allow a rescue, and it would be first light before any further attempt could be made. The news was devastating, and hope of rescue seemed gone. My stomach felt like it fell to my toes, and I quickly realized that I had been putting my hope and faith in the power of the United States and all the military forces available to them in this area of the world to rescue me.

I had accepted Jesus Christ as my Savior when I was in college through the ministry of the Fellowship of Christian Athletes. My spiritual growth continued through Officer's Christian Fellowship and Campus Crusade for Christ Bible studies. Because Jesus was the Lord of my life, I was aware that He was the only solid rock on which to stand. I cried out to God during this devastating situation and told Him that I did not want to die here and that I wanted to see my family again, but I would also accept His will for me in this situation. Calmness and peace came over me and remained throughout the night and even throughout my capture and the period of time that I was held as a prisoner of war. There were times that I was beaten and tortured and the situation was bleak, but that peace never left me. I realized that this was not of my power, but was supernatural power. God, not the circumstances, was in control of my life.

I continued to make contact with rescue forces throughout the night. Apparently the enemy had surrounded me, and a North Vietnamese soldier stepped on me. As I reached up to grab him, I realized that I was surrounded by about 15-20 enemy soldiers with AK-47 rifles pointed at me. The soldier took a club and began to beat me with it. I was beaten so badly that I was unable to use my arm for three weeks. When the beating stopped, another soldier grabbed my pistol out of the holster, held it to my head, and pulled the trigger. The weapon did not fire! Before he could pull the trigger a second time, another soldier grabbed the gun from the hand of the soldier who had tried to kill me. God was faithful even in the small details. I had obeyed the order to keep the first round in the cylinder empty, and that obedience and the grace of God saved my life. I was then stripped of my flight suit and boots, blind-folded, tied up, and walked all night with enemy soldiers to a bunker. It took almost one month to reach Hanoi, traveling by boat and truck. Most of the time I was tied up, handcuffed, or in leg irons. Two other POWs, including Ray, were captured along the way and were transported with me.

Once we arrived in Hanoi, I was placed in solitary confinement for a period of time and eventually was placed with three cellmates. The conditions were primitive, with poor food, some torture, and rampant sickness. However, God was ever present and gave us hope, peace, and strength. The pistol that did not fire was not the only miracle that happened in that prison. Scratched on the wall of my first cell in Hoa Lo Prison (Hanoi Hilton) was the statement: "Freedom has a taste for those who have fought and almost died for it, that the protected shall never know." I claimed the promise of God from His Word: "If God be for us, who can be against us?" (Romans 8:31)

When the peace agreement was signed and we were released to our countrymen, it was like a giant weight was lifted off me. The oppression of captivity gave me a fresh awareness of what true freedom is all about. While in prison, I realized that I had taken my freedoms for granted all my life and was determined upon my return home to read the Constitution and fully understand the oath that I had taken to defend it. After reading it, I learned that God and liberty are the basis and moral compass of the United States of America. The promises of "Blessed is the nation whose God is the Lord" (Psalm 33:12) and "Where the Spirit of the Lord is, there is liberty" (II Corinthians 3:17) give us a standard for our people and our nation.

The enemy was able to take away my physical freedom and to make me feel like I was at the end of my mental and emotional rope, but they could not take away my spiritual freedom, which was in God's control. I realized then that the rights and freedoms in the Declaration of Independence are God-given, not given by man. Thus, only God could take them away or we can freely give them up. Jesus said: "I will never leave thee, nor forsake thee" (Hebrews 13:5). I claimed the promise then and still do today. God bless America!

Colonel John Clark
U.S. Air Force (Ret.) • Vietnam

As we proceed through life, we begin to realize that we are less and less significant, and God's creation that abounds around us, often unnoticed, increases in its significance. Our successes, which are usually measured by personal and material accomplishments, will only transcend to significance when we are able to positively influence the lives of others. We also appreciate God's creation more as we realize that we are blessed to be part of it.

A quote engraved on a plaque I received upon departing the unit I commanded filled me with a feeling of significance: "Your wisdom and leadership inspired us to search for excellence." In life, we are all blessed with certain abilities and a free will with which to use those abilities. It is up to each of us to apply those abilities to the greatest good. A strict code of integrity and honesty in our dealings with others is a key to reaching success and significance.

While a POW in North Vietnam for six years and out of touch with the rest of my world, I mentally created a scrapbook of memories of family, friends, events, and things that pleased me, and I reviewed it frequently. In doing this I noticed and remembered things, of which I was not proud, that kept finding a place in my scrapbook. As years passed, my scrapbook became tattered, faded,

187

and some of the pages were missing. I came to realize that the memories that stayed the most vivid were the ones wherein I had made people comfortable or happy. Likewise, I noticed the memories that I regretted most were also slow to fade. I know from that experience and as I reflect on significance in the winter of my life, that my life will be measured by what I have done to cause happiness in the lives and souls of others. And I also know it will be measured by the suffering that I might have caused.

THE CROSS

I grew up attending a Christian church in the Midwest and remember well the various church socials and events that we attended as a family, my baptism, and my faith in God and Jesus Christ. As I grew older, matured, and pursued my college education, I noticed a divergence between the teachings of the church and the absolutes of scientific thought and discovery. As I followed my personal aspirations for life, I drifted away from the truth of the church and my faith with little consideration of its teachings.

Some years later I was shot down from the skies of Southeast Asia and a captive of the Communist North Vietnamese who desired information that I was reluctant to give. In short order, the torture convinced me it was time to call upon my forgotten faith, because this was clearly a situation where I needed a greater strength than I possessed.

I prayed and found my prayers hollow. I prayed with all my heart and found no strength, only emptiness. Clearly, my faith had waned. Over a period of gruesome days, I asked myself why had God left me so alone, but I knew the answer before asking: doubt and faithlessness had taken its toll. I had a choice—to endure alone or to find my missing faith and hopefully the inner strength that it might bring. I decided that even though the timing was rather self-serving, my sin would almost certainly be forgiven by an omniscient God if I were sincere in my search for true faith. So the journey began, the journey of rediscovery of faith. I thought perhaps an understanding God might give me a boost with a sign, and I promised in faith that I would try to recognize the sign. I really didn't expect a deep voice from the sky.

I was shot down in March, and the days were damp and cloudy. The cell was cold and dank, and there was a light drizzle in the air, which I could see if I stood on one of the concrete benches that served as a bed. The walls were a moldy, whitewashed stucco with numerous dates, names, initials, and other curious etchings. I noticed that some of the dates were from the French Indo-China period, and I could not help but wonder who of the French Foreign Legion might have shared a similar fate in this cell so far from home. I wondered if they had also betrayed their faith. Had they found the strength to endure an unknown fate?

As I lay on the cold, bare concrete trying not to think of my circumstance, I committed an act that was not allowed by camp regulations—I fell asleep. Some time later, I awoke with a nervous start. Had I been discovered by the roving guard outside the door? It seemed not, but more surprising was the wall at my feet opposite the high, narrow, barred window that was a stunning white, bathed in a dramatic ray of light shining through the small window. I quickly jumped up and peeked out the window, which revealed a bright setting sun. It slipped under a cloud layer just before it settled out of sight behind the imposing broken glass covered wall of the prison and the Hanoi skyline. So stunning was the patch of white, illuminated wall, that my attention was immediately drawn to it, and just as quickly, I noticed a perfectly etched cross in the center of the ray of light on the wall. I thought I knew everything that was on that wall! I had looked over every inch of it to discover whatever I could, and I had never seen a cross! I reasoned that I had missed it in my pained search, and now a setting sun just happened to illuminate it. Maybe that is why the Christian who etched it there did so. Or was it the "boost" that I had asked for, and would I, as I had promised, have the faith to realize it?

The inner stirring and the tears in my eyes easily conveyed my answer, and my journey back to faith continued with a prayer of thanks and the creation of a story that is still known only to God and to my heart. That cross became the center of my torturous stay in that cell, and it was only the first of several boosts, some not as easily explained. These signs were to mark my path to a new and re-newed faith and strength, which I credit for blessing me with a new life.

Colonel Carlyle "Smitty" Harris
U.S. Air Force (Ret.) • Vietnam

It is difficult to express a creed or code of conduct, which guides one's life, in a few words. Everything I do, say, act, think, respond to, avoid, or consider is part of my makeup that has been formed from infancy by heredity, family, teachers, role models, reading, experiences, observations, beliefs, religious upbringing, and sometimes attitudes which I do not know if they are learned or are a basic part of one's being. The following are not necessarily in the order of importance (which may change due to the nature of the circumstance) nor are they comprehensive.

1. I believe in God and an afterlife. I believe in prayer, but I think that God rarely responds to a person in miracles we ask for. Nevertheless, He responds with gifts much more valuable than we could have ever conceived. As a POW, the torture did not stop. I wasn't reunited with my family, the pain continued, time drug on, other sick men died. But eventually nearly all the personal miracles occurred—just not on my selfish timetable. But I gained in many ways—to the extent that I now believe the POW experience was very positive in my life. I believe I have a greater enjoyment of everything in nature and in life, a stronger faith, and feel good

about myself and my family relationships. I am optimistic and happy. I am better able to make good decisions. Whichever of God's character traits I may have, I believe they are stronger and less vulnerable to any temptations. I believe my prayers were answered.

2. I believe optimism and a can-do attitude are the attributes which are most important to the successful completion of almost any endeavor.

3. Integrity is one of the most important attributes one can have. Dependability and responsibility are just subsets of integrity. If one says he will do something, be somewhere at an appointed time, help with a cause, or carry out a project, failure to do so (except for impossible and unforeseen circumstances) is a direct and negative reflection of his integrity. For myself, I believe the worst thing that would destroy my self-esteem would be the knowledge that I had not told the truth or had failed to do that which I had promised to do.

4. Establishing good relationships with others (especially our family) is another almost absolute in my life. It makes me very happy to see my three children happily married, leading productive and happy lives, and instilling in their children the values which I believe are important. It is almost an affirmation that Louise and I must have done something right. Being kind to those who have no relation to me is also important.

My response to how to move from success to significance is as follows: Achieving my goals and having positive outcomes (success) is, of course, personally rewarding. Whether intended or not, what one does is observed by those with whom one comes in contact. If the achievements are considered worthy, good people will try to emulate or copy the manner in which the goals were reached. I would much rather make someone else feel important and significant.

During my incarceration in the prisons of North Vietnam, I was fortunate, even blessed, to introduce the tap code early on. This method of communication was very important to the entire POW group. I just happened to be the person, at the right time, with the right tool needed for communication. More importantly, I am a significant person to my wife, children (and their spouses), grandchildren, and close personal friends and that is the significance that I seek. And, of course, each of us is of great significance to God.

<hr />

WELCOME HOME, DAD

At two o'clock in the morning, the Air Force C-141 landed at Maxwell Air Force Base in Montgomery, Alabama. As I walked off the aircraft, my emotions were in total turmoil. I was about to meet my wife, two daughters, and a son whom I had never seen. It had been almost eight years since my F-105 fighter had been shot down over North Vietnam, and my son Lyle had been born one month later.

In Okinawa, Louise and I had purchased a very nice three-bedroom home with a fantastic view of the Pacific. About 75 feet from our large back porch was a steep bluff overlooking a small village below and Buckner Bay where a U.S. carrier and support ships often anchored. Our life was almost idyllic. Robin and Carolyn, ages four and three, laughed and played happily—often with our maid, Shiko, who was enthralled with their antics and their almost white blond hair. Louise kept busy decorating our nursery and making other preparations for the expected addition to our family. We did not know if we were going to have a little girl or a little boy, but it didn't really make any difference. Life was great.

The 67th Tactical Fighter Squadron was a very close-knit unit, including our wives. We often partied together, and the wives were a wonderful support for each other when we pilots were sent on temporary duty to Thailand, from where we flew combat missions over Laos and North Vietnam. Our Squadron commander, Lt. Colonel Robbie Risner, had been a Korean War fighter pilot, was a natural leader, and commanded respect for his living example of

Christian faith. For a young fighter pilot, it couldn't get much better than flying combat missions in a sophisticated fighter with other pilots whom I knew and trusted. We were well trained, capable, and knew that we were supporting our country's mission to keep South Vietnam free from the Communists of North Vietnam.

Then, on a bombing mission, my aircraft was hit by enemy anti-aircraft fire, and I was forced to eject and parachute into hostile territory. During my incarceration, my primary responsibility was to resist any efforts by my captors to exploit me in any way for their purposes. There were times when we were tortured, denied medical attention, malnourished, kept in solitary confinement, threatened, and made to suffer both extreme heat and cold. When things were really bad, there was a hierarchy of beliefs without which we could not survive. The first was a belief in God, then our country, our fellow POWs, and our family and friends back home. We simply must not let them down—and we gained strength to prevail over a brutal enemy by our firm foundation in these beliefs. No matter what our religious practices had been prior to captivity, there were no atheists when we reached the point where we were not sure we would survive. We prayed. Almost all of us gained the strength to continue and eventually came home with our honor intact. Unfortunately, there were some who were killed or could not survive their treatment.

My thoughts and prayers were never far from my family. From later shoot-downs, including Robbie Risner, I found out that Louise had given birth to our son, Carlyle S. Harris, Jr. (Lyle for short.) As I walked down the ramp of that airplane at Maxwell Air Force Base I was thinking over all the questions that had plagued me for the last week when I found out that we were going to be released. Had Louise changed? Would Robin and Carolyn remember Dad? And the biggest unknown was Lyle. Well, I was about to find out.

I was directed to a staff car and entered the back seat—in the dark, I had not been able to see inside—and there was Louise. She had never looked more beautiful. On the way to the Officer's

Quarters, she briefed me that waiting there were not only the kids but my Mom and Dad, my brother, Louise's mother, her sister and husband, Dick, and their children, and Louise's grandmother. I had hoped to spend a day or two with just Louise, perhaps in Hawaii, to catch up on all the family news so I would be better able to respond to them. But, this was exciting too. I was just bursting to see our son. As I stepped into the quarters, both Robin and Carolyn squealed and came running to jump in my arms. Oh, thank you Lord! They hadn't forgotten. They had grown to be lovely, young women—I was overcome with emotion and tears of joy rolled down my face. Then there was Lyle. I picked him up and hugged him for a long time, and it didn't bother me that he didn't hug back. I knew that would take a little time. Louise had always talked about me to the kids, and she said that when planes flew over, Lyle, even as a little boy, often remarked to his mom, "There goes Daddy." But the man picking him up was still a stranger.

I was, of course, delighted to see everyone. The whole room was almost chaos with talk and laughter. I had purchased gifts for everyone while I was at Clark Air Force Base in the Philippines, en route home. And they all had gifts for me. After about 30 or 40 minutes, while I was sitting in a large easy chair and opening a gift, I looked around for Lyle and found him in a corner just watching me. I turned and opened my arms toward him and he came running, jumped into my lap, and threw his arms around my neck in a big hug. Again, oh thank you Lord!

David Ludlum
Korea

I was released from captivity on April 20, 1952. In 1957 I went to South Korea to begin the first of two lay missionary terms helping orphans of the Korean War. For 18 years I supplied Christian books and Bibles to Third World pastors and schools. In 1985, I married a Filipino lady and eventually moved to the Philippines to work with churches there. My advice for life is: Love God and love people. Always treat others the way you want to be treated. God does have a plan for your life...be willing to submit yourself to His plan.

OH GOD, YOU'VE GOT TO HELP ME!

During the Korean War, I was in the Army, assigned to the 2nd Infantry Division, 38th Regiment, C Company of the 1st Battalion. I was captured by the Chinese Communists and became a prisoner of war on May 18, 1951. Twelve days later I was able to escape with a friend but we were recaptured after five days of freedom. Sometime around the 1st of July we arrived at "Mining Camp," (some called it "Bean Camp"). Two weeks later the larger group with whom I had first been captured arrived. It was not long before men in the group began to die from disease and lack of food. This continued throughout the summer.

One day I began to notice that my throat was swelling due to a tooth abscess. As the abscess increased in size, I was unable to eat or drink; even breathing was difficult. I was growing weaker by the day and on the 12th day I decided that I had to get up. I had a strong will to live but knew that if I couldn't get food and water down, I would die. That afternoon I stood and used all of my remaining strength to go outside—I walked about 50 feet. The short distance took all my strength and 30 minutes to complete. Outside I sat down on a rock and lowered my head in despair. A thought came into my head. I looked up into the sky and said, "Oh God, you've got to help me!" My eyes began to fill with tears as I lowered my head again. All of a sudden, a bitter-tasting liquid filled my mouth and I realized the large abscess had begun to drain. My prayer had been answered. I was once again able to take limited amounts of food and water, starting my road to recovery.

I was moved to Camp One Hospital, formerly a Buddhist temple. A Chinese doctor visited the room I was in and inquired about the small black books beside the bedmat of many of the patients. The book was the New Testament, given to us by front-line chaplains. I picked up my New Testament, stood up, and walked over to him and let him look at the small Bible. He looked at it briefly and returned it to me. Over the weeks that he came to visit, I began to talk to him. (I was being treated for beriberi and tuberculosis.) After his rounds, I often followed him outside to visit. He began to look up verses and passages in my New Testament. Up to then, I had not really read much of the Bible. After he left, I looked up the verses that he told me to find. Over time my faith began to increase and in December 1952, while at the POW hospital, I committed my life fully to God. I said, "Oh God, if you will let me return home, I promise that I will serve you for the rest of my life." By Christmas, I was too ill to eat the POWs food. About midnight the doctor came to my bedside and hand-fed me sweet cake and milk from his own rations. When I had gained enough strength to leave the hospital, he walked with me as we left the hospital compound. As we walked toward the camp headquarters, he told me to open my New Testament to Romans 13. He told me that he had seen a change in my life as he explained how to live a Christian life. Reaching the camp headquarters, I climbed into a truck. It seems strange to have become a soldier, to have fought in a war, to have become a POW and to meet a Chinese physician who not only helped save my life but also helped to direct me along the path to becoming a Christian.

Mark Moore
WWII • ETO

I was a nine-year-old child when, at an altar in a small church in Houston, Texas, I made a commitment to live for Christ. Later I discovered two short words that have been important guides in my decisions and actions.

One word is BE. This challenged me to "BE all that you can be!" I would not allow my actions, though sometimes short of my goals, to discourage me. "You can BE better than that," became a constant reminder.

The other word is DO. I cannot recall when I adopted the philosophy, "DO what you can, with what you have, where you are." However, these two attitudes have been faithful guides for me over many years.

THE PRAYER OF A SMALL BOY

After I completed Chaplain School on May 8, 1944, I was assigned to the 106th Division stationed at Camp Atterbury, Indiana. In September we began our move to England. On November 25, 1944, with black blinds on the windows, I knelt at the altar of a small base chapel in Gloucester, England. As I read the Psalms by the light that flickered from the fire in a small stove nearby, a portion of Scripture caught my attention. It was Psalm 66 that reads: "For you, O God, tested us. You refined us like silver. You brought us into prison and laid burdens on our backs. You let men ride over our heads; we went through fire and water, but You brought us out into a place of abundance" (NIV). I was so impressed that I wrote on the flyleaf of the New Testament, the reference, the date, time, and the words, "God's promise to me."

We were moved to Europe and up to the front lines of the battle replacing the war-tested Second Division. We were told that this was a rest area and that we would begin to get some combat experience here. However, on December 16, 1944, the Battle of the Bulge began. I was stationed at St. Vith, several miles behind the front lines. General Leo McMann, Commander of the 106th Division, wanted a Chaplain to go to the front to be with the artillery units supporting the two Infantry Regiments, the 422nd and the 423rd. I was selected.

I worked in the Aid Station praying with the wounded and endeavoring to comfort the dying. Rather than returning to St. Vith for the night, I stayed with the men on the front. By morning I saw the wisdom in staying with these forward units. The battle raged many days and nights. I was captured on December 19, 1944, at a time when we were completely surrounded and there was no hope of escape.

About 3,000 of us prisoners were being moved to Bad Orb in boxcars when we were attacked and bombed by RAF planes whose target was the Limburg railroad yard. Needless to say, we were all praying and hoping that the bombs would miss their target. My wife, Clarice, had written me many letters, some of which were returned to her. Among those returned was one letter that told a story about our son, Kent. Apparently while at church, he was tired and wanted to go to sleep. Before he laid his head in her lap he prayed, "Father bless and keep my Daddy and bring him home to me and Mommy." When I returned home, as best as we could place the time of his prayer, it was at the same time that we were being bombed. I believe the prayer of a small boy, and no doubt many others, reached the ears of God and spared us great tragedy.

We were bombed again on April 5, 1945, at the Nuremberg, Germany, railroad yards. I was put in charge of helping bind the wounds of those injured and also had to help with the identification of 24 American officers who were killed. Although a difficult assignment, it was a sacred privilege to secure one dog tag to the body and take the other, plus small personal belongings such as a billfold, watch, or ring and put them together in one of their socks to be delivered to the next of kin.

Near Gars on the Inns River we were liberated by the 86th Infantry Division. I asked one of the liberators if he knew my brother who was in the 86th. Captain Barney Slagle, a Forward Observer with the Artillery, helped me find my brother's room. We had a glorious reunion.

After a week I went to Camp Lucky Strike and on to New York. Truly God kept His promise for, "He brought us into a wealthy place." I have learned to "Do what you can, with what you have, where you are." Trust in our gracious God to be faithful. He will do whatever seems wise unto Him.

William Paschal
WWII • ETO

The experiences in prison camp profoundly affected and strengthened my belief in a power greater than man. I entered the Army at the age of 17, was trained, entered combat, and was imprisoned in short order. I was released from prison camp in Germany six months before my 20th birthday. As a young man, I did not have a deep faith or religious feelings, but I attended church, worshiped, and did the religious thing, because it was the norm for our family and our community. "Non-committed" would best describe the depth of my faith and feelings at the time.

I came out of prison camp convinced that God is everywhere at all times and is to be found by every living person as we reach out to accept His help. I was awakened by a strong vibrant voice speaking out in the black of night, speaking of hope when despair and hopelessness engulfed an entire prison of American POWs in Germany. We regained the power to endure and to live for tomorrow. The experience brought peace of mind and endless hope to those who had once despaired of hope and thought their life would soon be over. This lesson of life has stayed with me to this day.

THE SINGER

Things looked pretty grim at Stalag IXB, Bad Orb, Germany. When our column of prisoners of war marched up to the gate on February, 14, 1945, we could tell by looking at the prisoners inside the wire that this was not a happy place. They all looked gaunt and unkempt. One of the German-speaking prisoners in our group asked the guard at the gate, "What kind of camp is this?" The guard replied in a short, brusque manner. The American prisoner did not respond when his comrades asked what the guard said. Later the word got around that the guard had replied that we would all be dead from disease or starvation within six months.

Our group had been captured during the German offensive, "Nordwind," the sequel to the Battle of the Bulge. This operation started at midnight, December 31, 1944. Our tanks had been sent northward to break the stranglehold around Bastogne. Our infantry group had been mauled and literally chewed up by the Tiger tanks, moving almost unopposed through our position outside Rimling, France. Those of us who survived, surrendered on the morning of January 8, 1944. We had been cut off from our lines of supply for two days. Seven of us found ourselves not just surrounded but also out of ammunition, food, and water.

When we arrived at the gate of the POW camp, we had taken only one shower since leaving the States in October. I had only shaved twice in that time and had no haircut for the past 90 days. We thought we looked bad, but the guys that were already in the camp looked worse! Most of them had been captured around December 16th, during the Battle of the Bulge.

The camp barracks were stone for the first three feet, then a single layer of board the rest of the way. In our barracks, there was ice on the inside of the boards every morning from the condensation of the breath of the prisoners. There was no overnight fire allowed in the stove, so we froze at night. When it snowed, snow always found its way inside near the spot on the floor where I slept. We slept on burlap bags filled with wood shavings. Everyone soon contracted lice from these burlap bags. Even though it was the coldest winter of record in European history, the prisoners would take their pants, shirts, and underwear off during the day and smash lice.

Our morning meal was soup that was made from green turnip tops, sugar beet tops, or grass. This meal always gave us an almost immediate relief from constipation. Morning coffee (in name only) was made by boiling acorns or bark. The latrines outside were slit trenches with a log alongside. At night 300 men were locked in the barracks with a single, one-hole toilet and one water faucet. Toilet paper was unheard of. Diarrhea and dysentery were rampant. At night we shared a loaf of bread and about three boiled potatoes or a cup of turnip or rutabaga soup among six men. As the number of prisoners increased, we shared the same rations among eight men. The recipe for bread allowed for 20% tree flour or sawdust, sugar beet tops, and a small amount of rye.

During the day, we passed our time doing nothing—there was no recreation or reading material. At 5:00 PM each day we were locked into our barracks to endure another night, only to awaken to the same thing each morning. Within 10 days all of us newcomers could tell we were losing weight. When we arrived, our gear was taken from us. We had no canteen, cup, utensils, or mess kit. I ate and washed out of my helmet. I was able to carve a crude spoon from a small piece of wood.

Initially our talk was centered around when we would be liberated. After a few weeks, the talk centered around if we would be liberated. Some of the prisoners who were captured earlier began to die of malnutrition and typhus or similar diseases. Some of the men disassociated themselves from the rest of the group; they wouldn't talk; they stayed in bed and slept away the day and the night. They were the first to die. Over time, the attitude of the prisoners became pessimistic about the future.

One evening in early February, after we were locked in the barracks, I heard a strong voice from the dark, saying, "I will recite to you the 23rd Psalm," and proceeded to do so. Some of the men made catcalls and booed. I then heard the same strong voice begin singing hymns, first Onward Christian Soldier, then In the Garden, and Softly and Tenderly, followed by others. As he continued, the dissenting outcries stopped and were silent. Every night after that, night after night, I could hear that strong voice quoting Scripture from the New Testament. The soldier told us that if we believed in a higher power, we could endure, and we could make it. He exhorted us not to forsake compassion, not to give up hope, not to withdraw from life, and then he would lead the group in songs and discussion. I spent a number of days trying to find out who it was that had this strong voice that offered us so much comfort. I eventually met him. His name was Glen Schmidt, and he was a soldier from the 42nd Division.

On February 22, I was one of 89 prisoners selected and sent to another labor camp near Leipzig. Liberation followed, and I returned to my life as a civilian, went to school, married, had children, and pursued a career. Periodically I wondered about the men that I had known in prison, including Glen Schmidt. Glen had made a strong impression on everybody. I am convinced that many men are alive today because he brought faith, hope, and sanity to an otherwise insane and brutal environment.

In the mid 1990s, I began to attend reunions of my Infantry Division and survivors of Stalag IXB. We attended a reunion at the Holiday Inn, in Tucson, Arizona. After checking in, Marjorie, my wife, and I went to the hospitality room. When I entered the room I heard a strong and familiar voice. I walked over to the man, moved in front of him and said, "Hello, Glen Schmidt! I have always wondered if you survived the camps." Glen was showing people in the group an Army helmet with a bullet hole in it. Apparently, he and his teenage son had visited the Maginot line area in France, where he had been captured after a bullet shot had ripped off his helmet. His son found the helmet at the very spot where Glen was captured. During our conversation, I mentioned that I was a retired dentist living in Wichita, Kansas. An odd look came on Glen's face. He said, "In 1969, I retired from the Air Force at McConnell Air Force base in Wichita, Kansas." God works in strange ways...all those years and our paths had never crossed.

Alvar Platt
WWII • ETO

As you pursue your education, you will eventually be offered two possibilities about the origin of life.

1. There was a big bang millions of years ago, and following that, the process of evolution developed, and here we are. Those who adhere to this persuasion don't know what caused the big bang, and there are a myriad of other things missing besides the link. In spite of these difficulties, this is what is taught today in school as science.

2. The other premise is that there is a Divine Creator that put all these things together and created us. He came down to earth in bodily form and paid a ransom for us that we couldn't pay so that we might spend eternity with Him. You can read all about this in a book that is still a bestseller.

My advice for life is: Read the Book. I once heard Pastor E.V. Hill say, "I don't want to go to hell; there ain't no exits!" There are instructions in the Book on how to avoid going to hell. Some say BIBLE stands for "Basic Instructions Before Leaving Earth."

"MAYDAY" ON A MAY DAY

May 1, 1943, started out like any other day that we were alerted for a mission. We got up for breakfast, briefing and assembling our guns. I was a waist gunner—the position was the coldest spot on the plane. With both windows open and flying at a couple hundred miles per hour, there was always a nice breeze. On this day we had mechanical problems with our plane, and we figured we were going to miss the mission. There was another plane ready to go, but one of the officers was sick, so we took over their ship. We didn't even have time to change to our guns.

New groups were arriving daily and, as was customary, a new pilot would ride along as co-pilot with seasoned crews to get an idea of what they would be getting into before they took the full responsibility. Major Rosener, a commanding officer of a new group, would be flying with us as co-pilot. The target was one we had been to several times before in the 16 missions we had flown, so we weren't expecting any surprises. To hit the submarine pens on the French coast, we approached the target from land so the bombardier would have something to line his sights on. As we approached the target, the bombardier actually flew the plane using the bomb sights.

After we dropped our bombs, we turned and headed back out to sea, dropping down to a lower altitude below the enemy radar. Major Rosener came back through the waist, and I asked him how he liked the mission. Up until that point, it had been an easy one. He responded that he didn't think he would have any trouble making 25 like this one. He would change his mind before the day was over, for 30 minutes later we were talking in a dinghy.

Flying back we had to penetrate a broken cloud formation at about 6,000 feet and the group split up going through the clouds. We were at about 1,000 feet and the visibility was poor. We were flying in a diamond formation with several other planes. After leaving St.-Nazaire, we encountered strong winds from the northwest that had blown us back toward the French coast. We were still flying in a fairly heavy cloud cover when land was sighted. We hoped it was England, but when I got a glimpse of it, I recognized it immediately as Brest, France. Using the intercom, I called the pilot and informed him the land we had spotted was not England, but France, and it might be a good idea to get into a better formation. Before we were able to do so, we were attacked head-on by a group of German FW 190s, and we took several hits. We lost our pilot and one engine with the first pass and fell out of formation. When you get out of formation, you receive lots of attention.

The German fighters began making numerous passes at us from both directions. We were hit again. When I looked over, I saw that the right waist gunner had taken a direct hit and must have been killed instantly. I decided to put on my parachute, and, as I bent over to pick it up, it was blown out of my hand. I received shrapnel injures in my legs and also was hit by what I thought was a 30-caliber bullet on the outside of my right thigh exiting on the inside. I immediately sat down on an ammunition box, and in just moments, we hit water, and I mean HIT!

We had rehearsed ditching procedures on a regular basis. However, our problem was that we didn't know that we were going to hit water. The plane was on fire, and the smoke was so heavy in the cockpit that Major Rosener couldn't even see out. The wind that had blown us off course was creating swells that appeared to be about 40 feet high, making ditching a hazardous operation at best. The left wing of the plane must have hit first because it was folded back against the fuselage, blocking the window when I tried to get out. The fuselage broke behind the radio room and initially let in enough water to provide a cushion for me. I was immediately under water in a lot of debris. I could see light at the waist window, which I swam to, but it was blocked by the wing and I couldn't budge it. I have always been able to hold my breath for quite a while, but I was beginning to wonder when and where I was going to get my next one. Just then a large wave caught the wing and pulled it away from the window, and I was able to swim out and inflate my Mae West life jacket. As I came to the surface, I saw the tail of the ship sinking out of sight along with half the crew.

No one had had time to release the dinghies. One of them had been thrown out on impact, but it was so full of small shrapnel holes that we had to pump it continually to keep it inflated enough to keep the five of us together. When it would float to the top of a swell, the white cap on top of the swell would drench us. We took turns pumping for the rest of the afternoon, on into the night, and during the next day. We were eventually picked up by a French fishing boat with two German officers on board and landed at Saint-Malo, France. We were taken to an Army camp, given first aid and some food. I was then moved to a hospital for treatment of my wounds and eventually moved by train to Germany to begin my time in a POW camp.

As Paul Harvey might say, now for the rest of the story. My father was a preacher in California, and he prayed for me every day. On the day we were shot down, my father was going from his home in Ripon to his church in Manteca. He usually waited to get to church to pray for me, but on this day, he felt a profound need to pray for me; it was an urgent need so strong that he pulled his car off the road and prayed. I'm thankful that he realized the urgency of the situation because I could not have held my breath until he got to his office in Manteca. Neither of us felt this was a coincidence when we later compared our notes and checked the dates and the time. We realized that his urgent prayer was offered at the same time that we crashed. Coincidence, I don't think so...the story is similar to the story of the nobleman in John 4:46-53, "So the father knew that it was at the same hour, in which Jesus said unto him, Thy son liveth...."

Captain Charles Plumb
U.S. Navy (Ret.) • Vietnam

When asked to offer advice about success, I am reminded of the advice my high school football coach, Clancy Smith, a wounded WWI veteran, gave me. After the final game of a one-and-seven losing season, I said, "I'm sorry, Coach, I guess we're just a bunch of losers." I still remember his words, "Son, whether you think this team is a bunch of losers or a bunch of winners, you're right."

The next day I told Coach Smith, "I don't understand, what do you mean by 'whether you think you're a loser or a winner, you're right'?" He explained, "The difference between success and failure is you, and it's a choice."

I am an ex-Navy fighter pilot with 75 combat missions over Vietnam. If I had it all to do over again, I would stop at seventy-four. The Vietnamese cell I was in was eight feet long and eight feet wide. I could only pace three steps one way, then turn around and pace three steps the other. Inside this cell, there were no books to read, no window to look out, no TV, telephone, or radio. I didn't have a pencil or a piece of paper for 2,103 days.

I spent six years at the "University of Hanoi," and I received a degree in hard knocks. It was a long time to pace three steps in one direction and then three steps in the other. I would not wish it on anyone. I would, however, tell you it was the most valuable six years of my life.

For two of the almost six years I was a POW in Vietnam, I served as the chaplain to the POWs. I feel I must stress the importance of faith as a key to significance. Finally, if there is one single thing I validated in that Communist prison camp, it's this: Coach Smith was right! The difference between failure, success, and also significance is you, and it's your choice!

<hr />

FORGIVING THE UNFORGIVABLE

I was really angry—at my government for sending me to Vietnam, angry at myself for getting shot down, and angry at my God for not sending a miracle to rescue my co-pilot and me when our F-4 Phantom was shot out of the sky. And perhaps most of all, I was angry at the enemy for the torture and brutality—the sheer physical pain they had brought to my body for no apparent reason. I lay on the floor and bled and wept.

I had no idea at that moment in time the significance of my experience and the impact it would have on the rest of my life. In fact, I was convinced that the most value this time could ever have would be a period of my life I could someday forget! It would take months of anguish to teach me a vital lesson. And even today, having had many years to reflect on the experience, I'm still learning and growing from being a prisoner of war for six years in North Vietnam.

In some ways, my psychological response seemed to follow the Kubler-Ross model in her book, *Death and Dying*. I can track her five stages pretty clearly in my experience. I was first in denial, having flown that supersonic jet through the sky thinking I was bulletproof. I couldn't believe anyone in the world had a gun big enough to shoot down Charlie Plumb. (The pain of the first bayonet stab in my thigh quickly brought me out of that fantasy and into the next stage.)

Kubler-Ross's second stage, anger, is where I dwelt the longest and learned the most. (Remember it took me years to finally understand and appreciate all this.) At that time I really wanted to kill something or someone. And I felt totally justified in that feeling. After all, by any intelligent analysis, I was the quintessential victim of circumstances beyond my control; I was 24 years old with a new wife back home, a graduate of the Naval Academy with a great future ahead of us. Why me, Lord?

My formula for the most indelible lesson of life is this: $L=PT$. In order to Learn something, it takes a certain amount of Pain times a certain amount of Time. For me, this lesson took a considerable amount of pain for about three months until I could move on to the next stage. Kubler-Ross calls it acceptance. I chose to think of it as forgiveness.

An engineer by education, I tried to reason this through. First I started to consider the consequences of anger. It became pretty clear to me that no matter how much rage I could muster, I wasn't going to affect the outcome of the war (which had been, as a military guy, my primary mission). In fact, my wrath seemed to actually encourage my enemy. And in harboring all this vitriol, I was eating myself up from the inside out! Assuming I still had the choice, it just didn't seem very profitable to harbor any negative feelings.

So I found a new definition for anger. Using our secret communication system, a fellow POW gave me this anonymous definition: "Anger: an acid which does more harm to the vessel in which it is stored than to the subject onto which it is poured." But even understanding that, the next questions were the biggest: If I can't pour the acid on something, how on earth do I get rid of it? How do I change my attitude? How do I ignore the atrocities perpetrated on me and my pals? I found the answer to be a simple tool, sometimes easy to say but difficult to implement: unconditional forgiveness. It worked in the prison, and it works today.

I had been a Christian since the age of 13, but I didn't have a clue to the meaning of Christ's purpose on earth until my six years as a POW. Different from any religion I have studied, Christianity is based on unconditional forgiveness. That's what God's grace is to me. And that's what Christ requests of each of us.

And it isn't just forgiving our enemies, sometimes it's forgiving ourselves. This, in turn, gives us permission to step forward and move on with our lives. I'm convinced that we can imprison ourselves with guilt and self-doubt so that we become paralyzed. And those mental prison walls can be more restrictive than the ones of stone and steel I was behind in the prison camps in Vietnam. We set ourselves free when we forgive.

So the act of forgiveness can be a selfish one. (I think it's okay to be selfish once in a while.) Because if you can keep a forgiving heart, you can keep a healthy heart. So forgive the unforgivable...for the good of others, for yourself, and for your God.

Colonel Benjamin Purcell
U.S. Army (Ret.) • Vietnam

Life is God's gift to you. A life well lived is your gift to God. Every moment is precious and should not be wasted for there is no guarantee of tomorrow. So live, that when you die, your Lord will say, "Well done, good and faithful servant" (Matthew 25:23).

LIGHT TO MY PATH

In early April 1968, my POW group, which had been captured in South Vietnam in February, was being moved to North Vietnam along the Ho Chi Minh Trail. We traveled at night to avoid detection. By then my legs were covered with infected sores from untreated leech bites. Malnutrition, forced marches, diarrhea, and infections were taking a heavy toll on me. I could manage fine when I was sitting, but standing and walking were sheer agony. When I was on the ground resting, I was never sure whether I would be able to get up again.

One night was exceptionally dark, and I couldn't see to walk. For several minutes I stumbled along, tripping on unseen roots and rocks. Each ditch and rut in the road became a major obstacle. I felt tired, beaten, and almost helpless. I knew if I fell and couldn't get up, I was going to be shot because the head man had already given that order. I was no longer the confident, self-sufficient, infantry officer I had been two months earlier. I needed help. I needed a light, and that's exactly what I asked for in the simple prayer of a desperate man.

"Lord, I've got to have a light here, because I cannot see to walk, and I'm not going to survive this march unless I can keep up with the others."

I will always believe that what happened next was a miracle. Within a minute, the guide, who until now had been content to walk in darkness, turned on a flashlight and directed the beam right at my feet. He kept it there for the remainder of the night. Never before had God answered my prayer so dramatically and so soon.

"If you believe, you will receive whatever you ask for in prayer" (Matthew 21:22).

Roy Shenkel
WWII • ETO

My advice for life is: Read your Testament! These words were spoken to me during World War II when I was a prisoner of war. The words had a tremendous impact on my life, and the statement has directed my steps for 60 years. The scriptural reference is Psalm 119:105, "Your word is a lamp to my feet and a light for my path."

LORD, I'M YOURS IF YOU WANT ME

I enlisted in the Army Air Corp in October 1942 when I was 19 years old. I spent my 20th birthday as a prisoner of war. Initially I trained as an aircraft mechanic and gunner and was assigned as a right waist gunner on a B-17 Bomber to the 463rd Bomb Group, the 774th Bomb Squadron. On my fourth mission, on April 6, 1944, we were to bomb the marshaling yards at Zagreb, Yugoslavia. Approaching the target, we were attacked by fighters and hit by a rocket in the bomb bay of the B-17. There was a huge explosion, and the plane immediately burst into flames. At the time we were flying at 25,000 feet, so I bailed out of the aircraft at an altitude of over 20,000 feet. Due to the lack of oxygen, I passed out, regaining consciousness just in time to deploy my parachute. I hit the ground so hard that I broke my ankle. When I was captured, I was interrogated and sent to a hospital in Graz, Austria for two months. I eventually spent time as a prisoner of war in Stalag Luft IV in Poland and Stalag Luft I in Barth, Germany.

I was a POW for 13 months and one week. The winter of 1944 was the coldest winter on record. In the morning we had to stand outside for roll call in snow that was up to our knees. We only had a small amount of coal to burn to heat our building. The barracks were built on stilts so no one could make an escape by using a tunnel. The fact that the buildings were off the ground made them even colder. We were always cold and hungry. The Germans never gave us our full parcel from the Red Cross so our food was usually potatoes, black bread, which contained sawdust, and coffee made from acorns.

To keep the POWs from being liberated, many were force marched across Germany. I guess I was blessed to have fractured my ankle because it saved me from being in the death march. However, I did spend seven days and eight nights in a boxcar with 50 other prisoners when I was moved to Stalag Luft I. During the move, we received no food and very little water; it was so cold that my hair froze solid.

I was not a Christian when I entered the service. In fact, I now know that had I been killed in that burning B-17, I would have spent an eternity in hell. While I was a prisoner, I received a small Gideon New Testament in a Red Cross package. I still remember the words of a prisoner who I had never seen before and never saw again. He said, "Roy, read your Testament!" To this day I wonder if it might have been the words of an angel.

After I started to read the small Bible, the stories and the words took on a new meaning, and I found hope and faith. I still remember to this day the exact spot and the time of day when I walked up to the barracks, looked up toward heaven, and said, "Lord, I'm yours if you want me."

Rear Admiral Robert Shumaker
U.S. Navy (Ret.) • Vietnam

Paradoxically, I learned a lot about life from my experience as a prisoner of war in Vietnam. Those tough lessons learned within a jail cell have application to all those who will never have to undergo that particular trauma. At some point in life, everybody will be hungry, cold, lonely, extorted, sick, humiliated, or fearful, in varying degrees of intensity. It is the manner in which you react to these challenges that will distinguish you.

When adversity strikes, you need to fall back with the punch and do your best to get up off the mat to come back for the next round. A person is not in total control of his destiny, but you need to know what your goals are, and you have to prepare yourself in advance to take advantage of opportunity when that door opens. Some important tools on the road to success include the ability and willingness to communicate, treating those around you with respect and courtesy no matter what their station in life might be, and conducting your life with the morality and behavior that will allow you to face yourself...for in the end, you alone must be your own harshest critic.

THE IMPORTANCE OF HUMOR

You can sometimes find humor in the most bizarre circumstances, and that humorous moment can often sustain your spirits in spite of the unpleasant surroundings. Such was the case one time during my Vietnamese imprisonment. The food was meager and monotonous, and after nearly three years of solitary confinement, I could barley stand up without experiencing dizziness. The yearly diet consisted of three months of pumpkin soup, three months of sewer greens, and six long months of cabbage soup. You can imagine how weary one becomes after six months of cabbage soup. We were forbidden to talk to each other or make any sound and so, quite unexpectedly, during one of the noisy bombardments by American jet fighters and equally noisy Anti-Aircraft gunfire, I heard a distinctive American voice shouting. He was directing his message to the pilots (as if they could hear him). "Bomb the cabbage patches!" was his directive, and it brought down the house!

NINE FEET TALL

Two years before our release, the Vietnamese moved us into a central location and let us live together in groups of 75 or so men. Having endured solitary confinement, we were elated to be with other Americans. Nevertheless one Sunday, when we tried to hold a quiet church service in our cell block, the Vietnamese suspected us of sinister plotting and stormed the compound with fixed bayonets. As they marched off three "ringleaders," the remaining guys started singing "The Star Spangled Banner" with near-deafening volume. After six weeks of solitary confinement, the stalwart threesome returned. We asked one of them how it felt to hear the national anthem after nearly five years of imposed silence. Colonel Risner said, "I felt as if I could go bear hunting with a switch; in fact, I felt nine feet tall!" Years later, after our release, Mr. Ross Perot commissioned a sculptor to cast a bronze statue of Colonel Risner. It stands on the campus of the U.S. Air Force Academy as a reminder to cadets about what true courage really means. The statue is exactly nine feet tall.

HELPING OTHERS

Two years into our imprisonment, the Vietnamese were bearing down on us to make anti-war propaganda. One technique was to withhold food and water until the POW was compliant. At the time we were held in the old French movie colony we called the Zoo. We lived in somewhat large rooms in solitary confinement or sometimes with a cellmate. Through our tap code communication method, we knew that one of our group was getting the starvation treatment. A week without food or water makes a man really weak. One of our guys waited for the siesta hour and managed (only God knows how) to climb up to the ceiling which must have been 15 feet high. He opened a hatch, climbed into the attic, moved over to where the tortured POW's cell was located, and used a rope to lower him some food and water. The Air Force, and all of us, can be proud of Bob Purcell's effort to help a friend in need.

DOING WHAT'S RIGHT

It was Christmas 1968 and the Vietnamese had announced that they would receive and distribute Christmas gifts sent by POW families provided that they did not exceed two kilograms. When the guard came to my cell door with a package from my wife, I was overjoyed. But he demanded that I sign a receipt. "No problem," I thought at first, but the receipt stated the following: "I, (fill in the blank), criminal number (fill in the blank), acknowledge receipt of this package." "Whoa," I said, "I'm no criminal; I'm a prisoner of war." Well, I never received the package. I did get a letter, though, from my father. The date had been cut off and several sentences, phrases, and words had been excised with a razor blade. The letter told me of my mother's sudden and unexpected death caused by a brain tumor. The Vietnamese then indicated that I could petition Ho Chi Minh, that nation's leader, to ask for early release. "No thanks," I responded. You've got to do what's right because your conscience will haunt you forever if you don't.

Colonel Edgar Whitcomb
U.S. Air Force (Ret.) • WWII • PTO

Success is earned, not necessarily crafted. It is attainable by all persons of all means and backgrounds. The hallmark for success is quite basic: to be in service to the Lord and to use the gifts He has entrusted to each of us for that purpose. How this is accomplished, though, is of utmost importance. The values of honesty, integrity, work ethic, and the compassion of "Do unto others..." mark the way we approach and accomplish life's work. How well we combine these determines personal success. How well this is accomplished in the eyes of the Lord determines significance.

THE LIGHT

I guess all ex-POWs have a story to share; mine is different than most. After I completed my training as a navigator, I was assigned to the Philippines at Clark Field. Following the attack on Pearl Harbor, the Japanese attacked the Philippines. I was able to escape from the mainland to the island of Corregidor but was captured by the Japanese. It was during this captivity that I met a young Marine officer named Bill, and we planned an escape from Corregidor, hoping to eventually get to China and home.

On May 22, 1942, at about two o'clock in the afternoon, we left the POW camp with a work detail of about 60 men to gather wood for the fires back in the camp. While going through the pretense of gathering wood, we wandered far to the north of the group which had scattered in the search for firewood. The guard was paying little attention to us. We found an old foxhole and jumped in. We frequently looked out over the edge of the hole but saw no one looking for us. After a long time, the sun began to sink behind the western hills, but it seemed like hours before darkness came.

As the darkness surrounded us, we headed to the edge of the water and at about 8:30 we lowered ourselves into the water to begin swimming. It seemed odd that only six weeks earlier we had made our way across the small channel in a boat fleeing Bataan. It was only two or three miles across from Corregidor back to Bataan at the closest point, and we believed it would be possible to swim the distance in a few hours. After about half an hour, we appeared to be a considerable distance from the shore; however, the dark outline of the Bataan coast seemed as far away as ever. Off in the distance we could see a light, and we decided to swim toward it so we could stay on course.

After awhile it began to sprinkle, and the water was no longer smooth. As we continued to swim, a large black cloud came across the sky. As the rain began to fall harder and the waves increased in size, I realized that I had not been in contact with Bill for a long time. I looked all about me, only to realize that the waves were so high that it was impossible to see in any direction.

"Hey, Bill!" I screamed as loud as I could. There was no answer. Again, I screamed, "Hey, Bill! Where are you?" I shouted again and again as I looked all about. The wind was blowing, the rain was coming down in torrents, and the waves were breaking over my head. The terrible thought struck me that something had happened to Bill. He was lost, and I was alone in the middle of the north channel. I continued to tread water and shout for Bill, but I was convinced that he would never answer.

It was then that I realized for the first time what a foolish idea this swim had been, and I understood why others back in the camp had ridiculed the idea of swimming to the mainland to escape. The reason that we had decided to try and escape is because we were sure that we would die if we remained in the prison camp. Again, I yelled, "Bill, where are you?" At the same time, I realized that I was making no progress, although I was trying hard, but all I was able to do was bob like a cork in the big waves. Then I heard, "Ed!" I thought I saw a dark figure ahead and responded, "Bill, let's don't get lost again!'

He then said, "I wonder where we are? I haven't seen the light for a long time." "Neither have I," I answered. As we talked, we continued bobbing up and down with one big wave and then another. There was no use trying to swim; we were not able to make any headway, and we didn't have the slightest idea where we were and in which direction we needed to proceed. By this time, we had been in the water at least three or four hours, and we should have been able to see the Bataan coast, but the sky was black, and the sea was black. There was nothing to do but to tread water until the storm subsided. It was a long time before the storm began to slacken. Finally it stopped completely, and we were able to see a tiny light shining in the distance. It took almost eight hours to reach the Bataan coast and what we thought was freedom.

Humanly, we all need to set goals, to set a course, and to remain on course. Life's inevitable storms will come, and all may seem lost, but continue to have faith and never lose hope. The same is true spiritually: set your course on the Light, have faith, and never lose hope no matter the spiritual storms that overtake you.

Jack Woodson
WWII • PTO

Live life in such a way that your association with people, with God, and with our nation will be remembered with satisfaction. Strive to live a life with no regrets!

WELCOME HOME

My training as an ROTC cadet at the University of Oklahoma culminated in my being commissioned as a 2nd Lieutenant in the reserves. In April 1941, I was called to active duty and went to Fort Knox, Kentucky. I was then stationed at Fort Stotsenburg in the Philippines with the 17th Ordinance Company, a tank maintenance unit. All the training that I had previously received was only about winning battles. There was never a peep about losing them. We had heard about the code of conduct for those who were captured... "name, rank and service number" dictated by the Geneva convention.

We surrendered in April 1942 to the Japanese, but we were not prepared for the bestial treatment of the Bataan Death March. In January, prior to the surrender, we were put on half rations and then in April, quarter rations. Needless to say, we were not in good shape. Many were suffering from malaria and/or dysentery. Those who were too sick to walk were killed by bullet, bayonet, or beating.

I can close my eyes and still see those bodies every few yards along the road.

I had a small New Testament, which was an inspiration during my sojourn in Camp O'Donnell and at Cabanatuan. In September 1943, I was moved to Japan where I remained until the end of the war. In II Timothy 1:7 we read, "For God hath not given us the spirit of fear; but of power and of love, and of a sound mind" and in II Timothy 2:3 we read, "Thou therefore endure hardness as a good soldier of Jesus Christ." I also found great comfort in the Scriptures of Romans 8:28, "And we know that in all things God works for the good of those who love him, who have been called according to his purpose." And in II Corinthians 4:8-9, "We are hard pressed on every side, but not crushed; perplexed, but not in despair; persecuted, but not destroyed."

After the truce in August, our Air Force dropped food using red, white, and blue nylon parachutes. Some of the fellows made the four flags that represented the four nationalities of the men in the camp. What a sight to see the U.S., English, Dutch, and Norwegian flags rise to the top of the flagpoles. All we had seen for three-and-a-half years was the flag with the rising sun. If a flag burner would have appeared at that ceremony, he would not have survived!

We traveled back to the United States on a troop ship which was scheduled to arrive in San Francisco in the early morning. Everyone gathered along the rail of the ship shortly after daybreak hoping to see the Golden Gate Bridge. What a disappointment when we were met with dense fog—we couldn't see 50 feet ahead! Our spirits began to sink, but suddenly the fog seemed to part. Both ends of the bridge were still encased in the fog, but the center section was bathed in bright sunlight—what a welcome! I don't believe there was a dry eye in the entire bunch. We were home! We could see our families and friends who had agonized about us during our captivity standing along the pier. What a welcome...God bless America!

About the Author

Colonel Jim Coy (Ret.)

COL Jim Coy served as a medical consultant for the U.S. Army Special Operations Command. He served two years as the national president of the Special Operations Medical Association and as the national surgeon of the Reserve Officers Association. He served with numerous Special Operations units and served with the 3rd Group, Army Special Forces (Airborne) in the 1991 Gulf War. He retired from the military in 2001.

His military awards, badges, and honors include the Legion of Merit, the Combat Medic Badge, Expert Field Medic Badge, Flight Surgeon Badge, Airborne, Air Assault, and Israeli Airborne Badge. He has also received the Order of Military Medical Merit from the Army Medical Regiment and the prestigious "A" designation—the highest recognition of the Army Medical Department.

Jim and his wife, Vicki, have three children: Tim, Tricia, and Joshua. His family is extremely important to him. He has a vision for men becoming spiritual leaders and standing strong for their families.

Jim frequently speaks to community, church, school, and military groups across the nation. Jim and Vicki are staff with the military ministry of Campus Crusade for Christ (CRU).

CONTACT INFORMATION
www.agatheringofeagles.com
coyjv@socket.net

OTHER BOOKS BY JIM COY

A Gathering of Eagles
ISBN 1-1-58169-049-5

VALOR – A Gathering of Eagles
ISBN 1-58169-111-4

Prisoners of Hope – A Gathering of Eagles
ISBN 1-58169-177-7

Matthew A to Z + 2 (adult book)
ISBN 978-1-58169-276-1

The ABCs of Matthew for Kids
ISBN 978-1-58169-318-8

The Miracles of Jesus for Kids
ISBN 978-1-58169-351-5

The Parables of Jesus for Kids
ISBN 978-1-58169-378-2

JIM COY WAS ALSO A CONSULTANT
FOR THE FOLLOWING FAMILY NET DVDS:
Valor
Prisoners of Hope

Note: These two programs are included on the DVD attached to the inside back cover of this book. If the DVD is missing, please contact the publisher at jeff@evergreen777.com for a replacement.